About the Author

Why would anyone who's not totally insane take on a fight like the drug epidemic? The answer is simple and so human because it is the same reason we breathe.

In life, many of our fights come to us when we're not looking for trouble, when all we want to do is raise our children in peace and prosperity. In this life, you can have peace and prosperity for so long.

But things can change. The Bible is very clear: we shouldn't stay in our comfort zone. There is a time to live and die, a time for war and peace, a time to laugh and cry.

If you haven't had to make war or bury one of your children, you're lucky. Millions of us have lost friends and relatives because of drug overdoses and drug-related murders. This will take you out of your comfort zone and out of your shell, especially when it occurs over and over again. I would have loved to have never been in this fight.

It's been said that everything happens for a reason. As we get older, we understand this. Only God knows the future, and this is the reason He hides it from us. If we knew in advance about the tragedies that would happen, many of us would never walk forward.

I didn't write this book just for myself and my losses. No; I wrote this book because the American dream has become the American tragedy. The pain and suffering that happen once your child becomes addicted to heroin or other drugs will stop you from enjoying that new home, car or prosperity that we think makes us happy. It will take away your happiness at the blackjack table, if you're trying to escape reality in Vegas. It can destroy your personal relationship with your wife or husband. The things we take for granted, those we consider our sources of happiness, just won't matter. The desire to take that vacation to the Caribbean just won't be the same if we don't fight or intervene to stop it.

Losing a loved one to a car accident, cancer or heart attack —and you getting that dreaded 3am phone call—is a tragedy you could not have prevented. Losing a loved one to drugs is a different story; you have time to fight and save your child, just like you would if they were diagnosed in time with cancer.

Most Americans believe that using drugs is like a self-inflicted gunshot wound that the user can control. We now know that because of some people's genetics, even small amounts of exposure can unleash hell on your child; and they can't stop it. It's like them running into a burning building by mistake or out of curiosity. Little do they know that there are many ways in, and often no way out.

For me, growing up in a small town in Tennessee in the '60s—and hitchhiking to Dallas at 15, looking for a more prosperous life—was right out of a Mark Twain novel. The year was 1965, and I had just walked past the cemetery outside my hometown. Little did I know that many people who had not even been born yet would someday be buried in that same cemetery.

Once again, this is the reason why God hides the future. If I had known about the events that would happen a few short years later, I would have not walked any further. If I knew about the future, I would not have even gone to the next town, let alone Texas.

For this, I am glad. God hides the future; but at 15 years old, the world is such a beautiful place. We don't even consider anything but going forward.

In 1965, Tennessee was much like Mississippi and the other agrarian states in the south. It didn't have the affluence that you could find in places like Texas. Economic opportunity just didn't have its roots in Tennessee at that time in history. But the economic optimism, the positive attitude, was unbelievably a part of Texas. No matter which state you go to, you will never find more solid people than those who exist in the great state of Texas.

You work hard to put your children through school, to feed and clothe them, often to find out that you put them on the right track but they still end up on the wrong train. When something is killing your loved ones or friends, you will drop everything that you thought was important in life to pursue an answer. If we try, we might succeed; and if we don't try, there's never closure.

As I looked around the world, I realized that my story and losses were not unique. These stories and losses permeate every small, middle and large city in America; and I began to understand. I wish this book was only about me, the murder of my two sisters by drug dealers, and the loss of my first-born son and many friends. No; this book is about America's ongoing drug epidemic, with a diametrically opposite and unconventional truth that has been hidden and obscured for evil, selfish and political reasons. I'm talking about an epidemic that is about to get worse, if you can believe that. I wrote this book to inform you of how and why it has been perpetrated against America. As you read I will expose the truth and bring America back to a time in history when we weren't afraid to die—and maybe more importantly, not afraid to live.

Dedication

I am honored to dedicate this book to my sisters Dinah Lynn Baker and Carolina Baker; and my son, Mark Baker.

This book is also for the millions of Americans whom I've never met and who have died or were killed, without any explanations that made real sense.

I also want to dedicate this work to my parents, Edward and Agnes Baker; and to honor their memory. You would have had to have been there to realize what a solid, stable and great way of life I had growing up, with these two for parents. Their love and security allowed me to have a childhood in the rural south during the sixties that generated and inspired free thinking with respect for everything and everyone in life. This was an atmosphere that encouraged adventure, honesty and fairness with all human beings.

Table of Contents

Introduction

A recent drug bust in Louisiana netted a peculiar substance in a quantity never before found on the streets. The two men who were arrested picked the shipment up in California. Apparently, it was delivered to the docks inside a cargo container from China.

After testing, this strange substance turned out to be fentanyl. Fentanyl is a drug so powerful that ten pounds of it could kill everyone in a city the size of Houston, if properly dispensed. Fentanyl was designed for terminal ill patients with unbelievable pain, not for the healthy and young. It was designed to be delivered in a transdermal patch; but naïve opiate users are extracting it and shooting it like heroin, causing instant death.

We have turned the page and reached a new level in the drug war that has gone nuclear. This drug can undermine, incapacitate and destroy the United States in five years if the foreign nations that are delivering it have their way. It is not only 600 times more potent and powerful than heroin, but is also that much more addicting—if you don't die on your first foray.

This is bigger than even money; this is about defeating America and never firing a shot.

America's losses have produced an estimated five million deaths over sixty years in our nation alone. No, there isn't a headline in the newspaper telling you that a million have died; that would be too obvious. These deaths were slowly spread out over years so as not to expose the American people to the truth, and unite them. These deaths were directly or indirectly caused by drug overdoses, violence, accidents, suicides, and anything else connected to drugs. This killer comes secretly and silently through the night air, similar to the mist that killed Egypt's firstborn, like what you saw in the Ten Commandments. The reason for the deaths are all unique, but the same quiet and subtle poison still delivers a lonesome death in a motel or a dark alley.

To speed up the overthrow of America and to incapacitate millions, fentanyl and other drugs were selected as a weapon of mass destruction. America is always looking for an attack and overthrow attempts by foreign entities or governments, even a 9/11 or Pearl Harbor-style assault. Our enemies know this. What America doesn't know is that a subtle overthrow designed not to wake up or unite us as a people is already underway.

Political correctness—coupled with fake news reports, subversion of race relations, and the division of our people—has been facilitated by the drug epidemic, which is now saturating every neighborhood, town, and city from coast to coast. These items are merely a distraction that are prevents us as a nation from recognizing the real danger.

The helplessness, vulnerability, pain and suffering that millions of parents endure haven't been explained. Their children may have started using drugs, but their lives shouldn't have ended in death. If they were found with a needle in their arm and die from a drug overdose, they have suffered the same consequence as a convicted killer sentenced to death by lethal injection. Most Americans do not look at it this way, and reality can only be seen after the death of a loved one.

After reading this book, you will understand and know with absolute proof and clarity how they did not deserve that destiny. We will also explain to you, the American people, why many of these deaths are now politically caused.

Millions have died from crimes related to drugs, and who weren't guilty of murder and have never done drugs. Most users don't perpetrate crimes or even cause most of the damage they do to themselves, but it has become their penance. This is not to say they don't hurt other people because you can't hurt you without hurting those that love you.

Once addiction occurs, most can't be trusted; therefore, you cut ties to protect yourself. A large percentage of users who were your children, family members, or friends may finally die. People who are guilty of addiction and minor crimes do not deserve lethal injection, but millions have received it with no court date or sentencing. Unfortunately, when we feel great and we're young, we write checks on our bodies that will have to be cashed someday.

This book intends to open your eyes and make you aware of how unique, privileged, and important your life is. We will explain why and how drugs can place death into every cell of your body overnight. This epidemic of drug use not only kills the young and the innocent, it also robs them of the future. This is a future that is exploding like never before in science, and in ways never before imagined.

If you are looking for a children's book or a Disney story, do not waste your time or money on this book. If you are like millions of Americans who have children or have been afflicted by this killer, you better read this book. If you know someone who is deceased, jailed, or nearly dying as a result of drugs, knowledge is power. Don't count on your local or network news to protect you; everything you thought you knew about drugs is only half-true.

Most people who have tried to explain this epidemic are sincere, but sincerely wrong. This book is intended to save your life and point out the potholes in the road to save your children's life and make sense of those who have already perished.

Yet the most surprising information that you are about to receive will exonerate you to a certain level, but not completely. We will show that we are as much (and more) a victim than villain in the drug epidemic. We are still responsible for our behavior and the consequences that occur. We try to raise our children, hoping to produce a great person for society, only to discover later on that something terrible slipped by us. Afterward, we see them on the wrong track and traveling at the speed of death, and they cannot be stopped.

Don't believe CNN or social media; the truth is much worse than they can explain. America's drug epidemic, which started out with greed and money, has now become the most potent and powerful military weapon that our enemies possess. There will be no prisoners taken in this book; there will be no compromise on the truth. And yes, there will be millions who will be offended and angry at me.

To write this book and not expose the perpetrators, foreign and domestic, would be tantamount to assisted murder on my part as a writer. This work is also dangerous for me as a writer: the people, corporations, nations and organizations that I will expose are very dangerous characters. There are spiritual entities and forces that are at play, as well as businessmen.

This book is about America, and the many lies and cover-ups that have cost millions of us our lives. America is the envy of the world; there is no other country or countries on Planet earth that so many people aspire to become a part of. Our wealth and freedom, unparalleled in history, are the reasons why you're the target.

This will be an explanation that you have never heard, with a reasoning and a logic that are unbelievable and were hidden. This information will flow like a river of living knowledge, but with plenty of turbulence.

Let's get started.

Chapter 1

Pharmaceuticals: the Oldest Drug Dealer

If you are one of the millions who cry (and have no words, reasons or explanations) when looking at a photo, this book will help you. There are no words that anyone could ever say to undo your loss, but you deserve to know how and why this happened to someone you love so much.

To understand how we stumbled into the quicksand of time, death and the drug epidemic, we must look back to antiquity first; then at ourselves. We all need answers.

Don't freak out, but our story actually starts in the Garden of Eden. No, this book is not a religious or a theological book; but we will touch on the range of scriptures from time to time. It doesn't matter if you are a student or believer of the Holy Bible or not because it's still a great source of information and historical facts.

The oldest known writing in archaeological studies are the ancient Sumerian texts that predate even the Bible. The Sumerian location is considered the cradle of civilization known as Mesopotamia, where most scholars believe the Garden of Eden was. (This is now modern-day Iraq, Kuwait, and the Persian Gulf.) This was also where mankind's first use of the poppy plant—the source of heroin, morphine, opium, and all opiates that exist in nature—was first recorded.

The ancient Sumerians described it as the joy plant; their term for it was 'hul gil'; and it was cultivated for medicinal and, yes, recreational use. Keep in mind that this was 5,000 years prior to the birth of Christ, and would be 7,000 years in antiquity from today.

One thing you can count on in humans is that we are creatures of habit, and apparently always have been. There was no Walgreens or CVS back then; but the same ingredients, products, and problems existed even then. This doesn't rule out the probability that it may have been cultivated or found in nature thousands of years prior to even this time frame. But this proves that man was subject to the same laws of physics or just as human then as we are today, and were as vulnerable.

Just assuredly as man developed weapons in early history for war, the poppy plant would become a weapon to destroy other nations. Most people never think of it or know this; but thousands of years ago, in far-off lands like the Middle East, the Orient, Israel, and yes, Europe, people were dying from opiate overdoses. The drugs they were using were absolutely opiates, and they had no knowledge of what was causing their deaths. Eventually, they connected the dots.

The extractions made from the poppy plant would also be used in Egypt during (believe it or not) the era of King Tutankhamun.

Marco Polo's discovery of a better route to China and the Far East set up trade routes with China, introducing opioids and the poppy plant as a weapon of mass destruction to that nation. The Silk Road, as it was called in the 12th century, would be used by the Dutch East India Company to rule the world. This was the world's first documented account of globalization and control of nations.

Great Britain and the other countries in what was called the Western world at that time literally conquered China, and pushed the sale of opiates for opium to the Far Eastern world. This was the first drug war, and China became known as a nation of shame because their entire population was almost incapacitated by the use of this drug thousands of years ago. There will be more about this drug as a weapon of mass destruction and war in a later chapter.

Thousands of years later, the tables are turned. This drug has been weaponized, and is now being used on the United States. We are the recipients of this mass destruction by foreign nations in the form of heroin and the newest most deadly killer, fentanyl.

The word 'pharmaceutical' is taken from the Greek Hebrew word *pharmakeia*. In Biblical times, this word was usually associated with the casting of spells, sorcery, demonic spirits and everything evil.

After looking at the consequences that can happen in a person's life when using pharmaceuticals or heroin, one can see why this description could fit the outcome. Let's get one thing straight—America the pharmaceutical and medical industry are fueled by one source: money. But that isn't the only motive or force behind this evil epidemic of death. There are spiritual entities and entire nations dedicated to bringing down our country.

No amount of words or logic can exonerate us as Americans if we abuse anything; we control what goes into our mouths as well as what comes out. This is where deception appears, and it is perpetrated on the American public and pushed by professionals you have trusted. We are talking about the medical industry, which we have been taught as having our best interest at heart since childhood. This is the reason why as parents, we trust them with our children and our lives.

Ask anyone who is addicted to heroin. Most will agree that pharmaceutical pain pills are the genesis of their heroin use. This is the reason you, as a parent, must watch closely and be unbelievably discreet about your medicine cabinet and the medical care and prescriptions your child receives.

This is a tricky road because some people have a genetic propensity or biology to be more addicted than others. Rehabs and research centers would like you to believe that it is a personality trait more so than biological or genetic, so they will not concur with my analysis. The term doctors and rehabs like to use is 'addictive personality'; they push this narrative to exonerate drug sales. Their answer: more drugs to change your personality. They are part of the medical industry, which is the main player and the beginning of this epidemic domestically.

The next paragraphs are but just several ways out of hundreds that can lead you down the road to this addiction. When these happen, they could destroy you; but make the pharmaceutical industry even more wealthy.

When we have an auto accident or a fall at our job, the first thing we want is a doctor who can save our life. The doctor's records will back up our complaint about pain and suffering so we can get a settlement.

After an auto accident or any accident, the next things we do are consult an attorney, sign a contract, and go to another doctor that the attorney usually recommends. After all, we would be incapacitated if we have an injury and are unable to work and support our families. At the time, it makes perfect sense that we should be paid for this injury. That's called insurance.

After our visit to our attorney, we will be further educated about what the settlement would be predicated or based on. They will explain that the larger the medical expenses, the more time off of work, and the more pain and suffering that we endure, the larger the payoff will be. We will be sure to complain to our doctor about our pain; and demand MRIs, X-rays, sonograms and any and all therapies that insurance will pay for.

We are following instructions and making the cash register go ka-ching for the medical staff, but it gets better.

At this point, we (as an outpatient or inpatient at the hospital) will demand large amounts of pain medication because it substantiates that we have been hurt and are in pain. As a normal person in good health, we are not accustomed to pain medication.

Doctors, clinics, and the entire medical field know how the game is played when there's insurance or a lawsuit involved. They also know the attorney wants the medical bills to be as expensive as possible. This is music to their ears; after all, who doesn't want to make as much money as they can, especially if the client is telling you to charge more? (While these words are never really spoken out loud, sometimes the unspoken words resonate and mean more than others.)

We who have families can easily justify a $1,000,000 settlement because we are incapacitated and unable to provide for a spouse and kids. Attorneys often say the lawsuit would take only a few months, but sometimes they drag on for years. Life could change drastically after just a couple of months or years of drug use via prescription opiates.

Opiates have many negative effects on human beings and doctors fail to mention that, but we are about to experience it. It's not that doctors don't know addiction is likely; or that it can destroy intimacy, sound logic, a marriage and the family. But it just don't seem important at the moment. The doctor will not be the one taking the narcotics. Neither would the attorney.

Many doctors do become addicted; but in our case, we will be the one coached and prescribed the same thing that the ancients Sumerians used. The difference, of course, is that medical science has now synthetically re-engineered opiates, making cultivation unnecessary with the ability to provide all that is needed by the masses in a short time.

At the end of 2 months or up to a year—including therapies, X-rays, and hundreds of pills—we would be an addict. People, especially the younger ones, do not look this far down the road because wisdom comes later in life. Before it's over, we would wish we had taken a small, meager settlement; gone back to work; and still have our health.

This scenario doesn't pertain to all injuries, lawsuits, or settlements. It's when frivolous or fake injuries have to be falsely generated that we get in trouble. This is where words will not exonerate us because this time, greed and deception are our fault. It does give us another good reason to be honest.

The promise of a $1,000,000 settlement is the enticement for us as a patient and as a client. The attorney will simply act on our human nature and greed; the medical field will finish us off with drugs after that. The greed that took us down this road, the love of money, is why we're now addicted to drugs.

This is the same selfish allure that causes millions to sell drugs. Only now is the pharmaceutical industry trying to take the high road after millions of deaths. In reality, this industry is really frightened about its exposure and liability to the American people—and lawsuits like never imagined.

After losing work for a year, probably our marriage, and setting a bad example for our children, it gets worse. This doesn't include our addiction or the change in our personality that won't be for the better, and makes us a liability to employers. We now must pay for our medical bills, attorney fees, and missed months or years of work. When the insurance funds are dried up and the doctor let us go as a patient, he will quit writing prescriptions—especially those for the opiates we are now addicted to.

If you are like 90% of the people who have experienced or experiencing this exact scenario, your health will have suffered more from the medical industry than the car accident. Remember this scenario doesn't have to materialize just because of an accident. A visit to the dentist or a doctor because of a migraine could now be the start of addiction.

You'd like to think that this is as bad as it gets and you're addicted only to pain pills, but it can and usually gets much worse. In America, the cure for opiate addiction is only about

5%; the other 95% either die, go to prison, or live out a shorter life as addicts.

We mentioned earlier that some people have a greater propensity to be addicted than others. This is the perfect storm caused by greed, and how the medical and pharmaceutical industries have fueled this epidemic. The small amount of money (or even a few thousand) that you'll finally get will be mismanaged, squandered, and wasted on purchasing street drugs.

There will be a much different you left living in a dangerous world with street dealers and shady characters. You will now be in a world defined by death by overdose or gun violence. If you turn to heroin in desperation, there will be no clinical measures and no guarantees of safety; and your life will be in jeopardy every day. Yes; heroin is a street substitute for pain pills, morphine, and any and every opiate you can buy.

There will be something else different about you that did not exist before your accident, and that involves your logical thinking. Opiates cause a glossed-over effect that makes the world around you appear much better than what it is as long as you're under the influence. This creates a laid-back 'whatever, I don't mind' attitude that permeates all of those who become opiate addicts. Of course, this means you don't see the world for the way it really is; you see it through a filter or strange prism, making you vulnerable. You will be bad in business deals and a poor manager of money as a result of this new you.

We mentioned earlier that opiates also destroy intimacy. This means your marriage or your relationship would probably be dissolved.

Since heroin is a biological substance synthesized by the medical industry to create pain pills, you are now back to antiquity. This puts you right back to where mankind was thousands of years ago, and it completes the circle of death.

At this point, you might as well tell the truth. After all, you've lost your health, your finances, your job, your spouse and kids. Most people wonder if they should have just settled and not been selfish; to be fair, it's not all their fault. This is the reason why the pharmaceutical industry is so profitable, and why a Walgreens or a CVS is being built on almost every street corner in every town.

Of course, the pharmaceutical industry did not stop with just synthesizing and pushing opiates. Watch any T.V. program, and you will see the airways flooded with commercials; most of them are pharmaceutical ads. These ads promise everything from weight loss to cures for sexual dysfunction. There commercials will promise a new lease on life, to fight depression, and to make life better.

If all of that wasn't enough, there will be another set of commercials that will flash in front of your eyes that are unbelievable. It appears that attorneys have found a new way to make money: by suing the medical industry, which has been their co-conspirators in lawsuits for years. Look at the commercials again. You will be asked if you have ever taken this or that drug. This is to get you to sue the pharmaceutical industry for any drug that has caused complications. This can be everything from blindness, impotence, or death. The ad will then be followed up by an attorney's name and phone number. It would appear that these two partners-in-crime are either still conspiring and playing a new game, or they have turned on each other.

Now that we are a nation of addicts, we have changed our personalities and our logic. You, once a good and solid working American with a family, are now considered a threat by police departments if you have a history of drug use. The police in America have developed a strange, ambivalent attitude about its citizens. They see the majority of people in 'us versus them' terms; this means they feel threatened daily by millions of people. They feel that there's a target on their back. This has created a wedge of hate and animus between law enforcement and the population.

And don't forget the millions they have been forced to arrest. These arrested millions (some, for just minor offenses) have a black mark on their record, and are tainted to a certain degree. Don't be naïve, America. The drug cartels, street dealers, or the medical and pharmaceutical industries don't care about your relationship with law enforcement.

This book will restore with clarity and balance who is responsible—and it's not you or law enforcement. From an economic perspective, police, jailers and all judicial professionals will have new careers if we all stop using drugs. More on this later; but just like doctors, I would never paint all in the police force with the same brush.

The allure and the pull of opiates is so strong that it will make you do things you would have never considered before your addiction. I suggest that until the epidemic is defeated, you as a citizen must cooperate with law enforcement at all times. Don't be afraid to communicate with them; let them know you are on their side.

Make no mistake, America. Other nations who push heroin are well aware of America's pain-pill addiction. These countries also know that as the pharmaceutical industry is forced to quit selling pain pills, you will turn to heroin as a substitute. The industry is now competing for your money, much like street dealers. One or the other will fill your prescription, legally or illegally.

This has been called the war on drugs or the drug war, but it's really a war on the American people. This war is perpetrated by our own domestic industry and foreign nations, but now it fuels our economy in a very negative but effective way. If there were no drug sales tomorrow, we would suffer immediate financial collapse in our country.

In the following chapters, we are going to look deeper and explain why countries like China, Afghanistan and others are using opiates to destroy this nation. For decades, China has been very dishonest in trade practices as well as the theft of American ingenuity and industry. Cyber hacking and the theft of our trade secrets, prototypes engineering and industrial knowledge are constant. We will expose their motives, and why America has allowed this to occur for the last 60 years.

After you read this book, if you are a red-blooded patriot (and most of you are), you should be fighting mad.

Chapter 2

Our Time Machine

There has always been a fascination in the American mind and science with time travel. For decades, H.G. Wells intrigued young Hollywood with this idea, as well as UFO invasions. Time travel would enable you to escape reality. While this technology isn't available yet, there is intrigue all around.

The modern world as we know it is set for you, as a human being, to see technological and scientific changes that even Hollywood's greatest science fiction writers could have never imagined. What is about to happen on Earth will be greater than any movie, book or video that you could have ever envisioned. The technological breakthroughs and achievements that you will miss if you die too soon is a good reason to hang around, if for no other excuse.

In your lifetime, if you are at least between the ages of 10 and 90 (and most of us are), you have seen the mapping of the human genome. Those of you old enough to remember the forties and fifties have witnessed America's change from an agrarian farming society to a much more urban and heavily populated country. In only 60 short years, this planet has made the leap from having almost three and a half billion to nearly 8 billion inhabitants.

These 8 billion people are embraced by globalists, giving them more customers in the masses to sell products to. Most of these products are made in third-world countries that spew out pollutants, particulates and gases, which cause climate change. If global warming is really occurring and man is the cause, it is due to overpopulation and materialism.

This is why globalists don't want borders; they want the masses contained in one simple world with one currency to make selling easier. Globalism has produced a more competitive world, and some will stop at nothing to be successful.

Now, new weapons are being used against entire nations. Some strategists believe these weapons are capable of creating drought; earthquakes; hurricanes; fires; and most importantly, addiction. Your very existence is in danger because of these world-class businesspeople, as we will expose in the following chapters.

Within 100 years, America has gone from the Wright brothers in Kitty Hawk to lunar landings and space telescopes that can see millions of years into the past. I say 'the past' because the vision, light or image that we are receiving now may have left some of these destinations billions of years ago. We are seeing those images as they were then, and not as they are now.

We are seeing advances in science that include every human being on the planet having cell phones, and SpaceX and NASA working together for launches and resupplying the International Space Station (ISS). There have been so many breakthroughs that many have forgotten that we are now capable of replacing vital organs like the liver, heart, lungs and kidneys. Many are still waiting for the final frontier: bringing the dead back to life. This means our bodies are now similar to our automobiles. In other words, if a battery, starter or windshield wiper blade goes bad, we replace them. Now, our body parts can be replaced in much the same way.

For almost 70 years, science has been busy in the world of cryonics, freezing people's heads in the hopes of reviving them later through DNA and genetic research with the same mind. The goal is to bring back the original human with all of his or her attributes, including love and recognition of their loved ones, still intact. I surmise this will never occur, and it is a counterfeit attempt at resurrecting the dead that leaves out God's role in life.

I also surmise that if they did bring back a small amount of life to a dead piece of biology, the most important ingredient that separates it from a cactus, a turtle, or any other life form isn't biology at all. More on this statement later.

As science seeks forbidden knowledge of other dimensions, scientists from around the world are at the European Organization for Nuclear Research (CERN) in Switzerland. These scientists come from every nation, and are all on the same page: to look for the secrets of the universe. They are smashing atoms at the speed of light in the Large Hadron Collider, the largest ever built on Earth.

Much like the fears with the first atomic weapons, when scientists claimed it could ignite the Earth's atmosphere, these scientists are treading where angels fear to go. Some scientists believe they may accidentally create a black hole with an appetite that could devour our entire galaxy. If they are successful and find what they are looking for, you will have answers in a few short years that may have been better off hidden.

Ironically, this research has been tainted with the proposition that it was influenced by supernatural and evil entities at its conception. There are rituals practiced at CERN by the staff and personnel that honor and dedicate their efforts to Shiva, the Indian god of destruction. CERN is looking for a new dimension using the comparison of us as humans suddenly realizing we are like fish in water, and that there are other dimensions to be explored.

CERN is trying to open up a supernatural world it calls science, but many theologians prefer that spiritual matters be left up to God. Theologians, pastors, and even paranormalists believe that CERN will open a portal into a dimension that will unleash demons in these last days.

Silicon Valley, China, Japan, and research centers around the world are producing nanotechnology. They are working night and day to create artificial intelligence. Some say this has the ability and the danger of replacing humans, then taking over the planet. But the positive uses of artificial intelligence could be used by the military to go into battle, or travel the distances in space that no biological species could endure.

Now that the global population is approaching eight billion, we are forced into new research to heal the millions who live in close quarters on a crowded planet. Many of these diseases that we are exposed to didn't exist half a century ago because they were obscured and thought harmless, or we didn't know they existed. As humans live closer and closer in proximity to one another, more diseases will be more effective in killing millions. And as these pandemics and epidemics develop resistance to our last lines of antibiotics, we are losing the race.

This scenario is more likely to occur now as we are packed wall-to-wall and back-to-back like sardines. Tropical diseases and climate change have caused a list of diseases that have never existed before. Many of these diseases have killed their hosts without ever identifying themselves.

Many of our resort areas, either in Florida or the northern states, have pestilence and dangers in their waterways. It isn't safe to go swimming in many parts of the South because of flesh-eating diseases or small microbial insects that can enter through any human orifice. Once inside the brain, it's almost certain death by these parasites or insects.

In other parts of our country, ticks or fleas that reside even in pristine, cooler forests deliver illnesses like Lyme disease that could kill within a week. Methicillin-resistant *Staphylococcus aureus* (MRSA) as well and other strains of influenza are at the precipice of contagion from animals to people, like birds to bird flu or bats to the Ebola virus. The only thing that has prevented the death of billions of humans is that the outbreaks have been addressed and contained in specific areas of the world.

Our food supply is also contaminated quite often by E. coli that can also kill in a short period of time. Science and research are trying to stay ahead of these pandemics and epidemics created by overcrowding.

As a nation, we are vulnerable to bioweapons that can be unleashed by terrorists that would spread quickly in this country and around the world in days. This fear was given credibility recently by Bill Gates in a world health conference, where he stated that viruses, especially flu viruses, could kill millions next year alone.

Research is going on 24/7 to stay ahead of these killer viruses that mutate and replicate in a different form each time they come into contact with our latest lines of medication or antibiotics. There has been an explosion of knowledge and research, more so in the last 50 years than in the last 50,000. The sum of all knowledge is being doubled almost every 5 months. Yes, a million years' worth of acquired knowledge is now appearing every few months. To say that knowledge is quantum now is an understatement of an enormous magnitude.

Microbiologists work in laboratories around the planet 24/7 to stay ahead and counterattack some of these microbes. Diseases that have the capability to annihilate billions worldwide and millions in the US are now possible. It is also a fact that in the last 13 years, the world has had an inordinate or suspicious amount of deaths among microbiologists. There are many intelligent people who believe that the deaths of these scientists occurs when they are about to expose a man-made danger that could kill millions.

Not only is the objective of science to beat these microbes at their own game and to cure diseases, it is also trying to give us up to 200 years of longevity. This research will include good looks, which is of course fueled by money, vanity, and the desire to be smarter. To look better, feel better and live longer is the catalyst behind health clubs, vitamin shops and cosmetic sales. None of these things are bad unless you die from a drug overdose after your operation or your plastic surgery from pain meds.

Tampering with millions of years of biological trial and error has created doubt as to whether we are more healthy or not. If that last statement makes it appear that I am endorsing evolution, nothing could be further from the truth.

The process of evolution versus the theory of evolution are two different narratives. Darwin's so-called theory left out the possibility and probability of divine intervention in creation. His theory suggests that if an event happens enough, it will evolve into a better species. If this were true, you could dump a load of scrap iron from a big truck for millions of years; and it would finally fall into a new car. Of course, we know a Corvette is a Corvette because it was created by man as proof of biological enhancement that no other species contains.

Without getting into a war of ideologies, it's obvious that there is more evidence to support supernatural creation. For those in doubt, we can say at least that biological intervention by superior beings is our faith or fairy-tale of beliefs. The evidence not to believe this requires more faith, and less seeing to believe.

We will take on that mental challenge later on in this book and explain the connection between it and death by drugs.

In a few short years, our world is at the precipice of breakthroughs that have not even been announced, but are about to be game-changers in the world of biology as well as nanotechnology. These achievements in artificial intelligence offer different understandings of the universe and physics, and will be revolutionary.

The ultimate goal of science is not only to make us beautiful, healthy, and disease-free; research is also trying to make us all wealthy and materialistic overnight. That same science can cause us to all be annihilated overnight. The only way you will ever know how this scenario pans out is to live as long as possible. Will science do us in, or will it make us almost eternal? Why would anyone want to give up their seat in this theater of life?

Even if you have damaged your body and your long-term diagnosis is bad, it's not too late to save what's left of your life. You can extend your existence for as long as possible as new research is occurring, and new cures are materializing constantly. They offer solutions to addiction and disease.

As long as you are true to yourself, admit to your drug problem, and are willing to fight, you have a better than 70% chance of surviving. If disease caused by drugs forces your exit and death occurs, it's game over.

This book is about drugs. It will connect the dots that you will miss in every category of life if you die of your own addiction. We will bring such interesting conjecture that it is very doubtful you will continue doing drugs after reading this book. Even if you do continue doing drugs after reading this book, you will most definitely seek help.

The objective is to open your mind to a world that you have not yet lived long enough to enjoy or remotely understand. By unleashing and allowing your mind to roam free, you will be addicted to the truth instead of drugs. While revealing the truth, we will also expose the reason why many turned to drugs to begin with.

You are about to be armed with unconventional knowledge that will make you a proponent of sobriety. This knowledge is being delivered to save your life and the lives of those you love even more than yourself. It will be a trip into uncharted waters that you cannot find in church, Facebook, school, or CNN. This is the power of the pen and the mind. It will demand that you strap yourself in for the mental rollercoaster ride of your life.

As you read these words and apply them to the world around you, there will be no doubt this is your time in history. We must also think unconventionally to save our loved ones on drugs and to make them see this. This is a very tricky and dangerous road because there is something that occurs in the human mind with a drug user. When you try to take drugs from someone and if they think you're effective, you will be considered a threat. Your threat to take their drugs and to change their friendships is a change they will resist because they have built their entire social existence around drug connections. Quite often, the human mind tricks the user into using twice as many drugs if they believe their source is about to be stopped. It will be at this point where the desire to do more drugs will permeate their thought process.

When you turn to friends for advice and wisdom, the most common answer would be that they won't stop until they are ready, or until they hit rock bottom. The problem with this logic is that we have discovered so many times that 'rock bottom' has been the grave for millions.

There has never been an epidemic, sickness, disease or affliction that begs to be prevented more than this one. This is the same logic that tells you in advance that your child should not play in the street. In other words, you stop them rather than pick them up after they have been hit and killed by a car.

Unluckily for me (but luckily for you), I have been through almost every scenario known today for this epidemic concerning loved ones, friends, and acquaintances. The knowledge and wisdom that I have garnered in the last 35 years of my life have come at a terrible price, and were paid for by the blood of innocent people.

When young people dabble in drugs, they do not think; nor do they have the knowledge that someday, maybe only in a few months, their lives would be altered and they could be close to death. This creeping, unknowable, and slow process of events for young and naïve people is the enemy's greatest tool of destruction and acceptance. Once addiction occurs, it's quite often irreversible because what was social play becomes human addiction. We will lift the veil in this book and arm you and your loved ones with knowledge to destroy the enemy's use of deceit.

After saying all of this, I would like now to board our time machine that will take us to a time in America when the masses were not addicted to drugs and have not died by the millions.

Recently, scientists as well as many astrophysicists and even NASA engineers are beginning to think of time in different terms. The thought of time being linear, the same way we think of a highway taking us from point A to point B, has changed. As logic changed, it was the first step to make time travel possible someday.

In other words, we don't necessarily have to travel in a straight line with time being behind us, much like the highway is behind us after we travel it. We're going to look back in time or back down the highway where we were before millions died because of drugs.

Our leaders in Washington have kicked this can of death down the road for too long, and now it's a pandemic and has the capability to destroy America. In fact, it has already afflicted and destroyed millions of American families. When families are destroyed, you also destroy a nation.

Let's get back to fun and physics and, of course, hypotheticals. Every generation has a flashpoint that, if they could go back in time, they would like to revisit for historical clarification, or to set the record straight.

My generation—those over 60, the baby boomers, the children of World War II—are fascinated by the death and assassination of John F. Kennedy. Most Americans will agree and concur that there are still some things that we do not know of or are either hidden or lied about regarding the murder of this charismatic leader. Around lunchtime in Dallas, Texas, on November 22, 1963, shots rang out at Dealey Plaza that would never be forgotten. Hardly any other subject has generated as much fascination, speculation or conspiracy theories as the death of this young president. There have been inquisitions and investigations by the Warren Commission and others that gave empty and unsatisfying solutions to the American people. Millions of us, myself included, would love to be a fly on the wall at Dealey Plaza to see if there really was another shooter.

In order to find this out, we would have to time travel backward. Naturally, after our visit to 1963, we would require the ability to return to our loved ones in the present day and report the truth. In 2019, we are even more suspicious. Many documents and findings related to Kennedy's assassination have been made public (The Assassination Archives and Research Center), but some documents will be withheld until 2021 due to "national security concerns" (Shapira, 2018).

Of course, there are many other things that we would discover about our society during this time if we spent time in the '60s. The culture shock of leaving our current time frame and going back to the '60s for a few days would not only give answers about that assassination; but would also let us see what people ate, how they dressed, and what their character was, as well as thousands of other items that have obviously changed by now.

You would not find as much political correctness; you would find more kindness, more honesty, and less deception. The reason why you would not find political correctness like today is because we didn't split hairs to make a point. Most people, whether minority or majority, put America's interests ahead of their own sensitive insecurities; and they weren't as defensive. Of course, this is not to say it did not exist; but it was pale in comparison to today's social indigestion.

At this time in American history, a man's handshake wasn't just a cordial greeting. A handshake meant honor; and if you didn't have that to many, you weren't a man. There's nothing wrong with today's paperwork to get a receipt, a title to your car, or anything legally documented. We all want to make a legal deal with tangible proof, but there is a missing dimension of honesty and honor missing in business today. Of course, there have always been shady characters throughout history. But the entire population, for the most part, wasn't corrupt from the top down.

There was no CNN or Fox News; no cell phones or computers for the masses. Medical science was antiquated and almost ancient by today's standards. Advances in medical science such as cancer research and heart and organ transplants don't exist yet, and we have not yet mapped our DNA.

Because of Kennedy's assassination, Dallas was stigmatized for many years and considered an evil city, with no logic to confirm this thought. America was also at the beginning of the Vietnam conflict. We were conflicted and felt as though we were compelled to fight in order to stop communism. In Southeast Asia, we faced what would be later termed as a 'domino effect' that could allow communism to permeate the entire planet.

Sadly, after thousands of soldiers have died in several wars to stop communism, socialist and communist ideas are growing in America in the year 2019. Yes the so-called millennials and many graduates from top-rated universities are more willing to throw away democracy and capitalism to embrace socialism. The sad part is this only speaks volumes about the people who are teaching in our universities. I also surmise that a trip to Cuba, China, or Russia for 30 days for each of these would-be revolutionaries will change their attitude.

We will really never know if communism would have spread then, but obviously it did not happen. Instead, freedom prevailed; and in my mind, that justified the Vietnam War.

60,000 Americans lost their lives and were never given the recognition they deserve, but it's not too late.

It is also true that many of the Vietnam soldiers came back with a bigger problem: heroin addiction. The drug culture and epidemic had not affected the masses at this point in history. It was just beginning at this time of the Vietnam War.

During this same time in history, African Americans struggled for equality, a struggle that materialized in every city. America, to say that blacks have not been denied equal rights would require you to live on another planet.

Of course, the epidemic of crack cocaine, heroin, and meth and amphetamines still didn't exist; but we're getting close.

In the '80s, dozens of highly dangerous designer drugs that are available today were at their beginning stages, but had not yet affected the entire nation. It is true that cocaine and heroin were available, but they weren't as plentiful as today.

We use the early sixties as a flashpoint for a good reason: it was at this point in time when America was about to give birth to the drug epidemic. Pharmaceutical methamphetamine known as 'black mollies' were given for weight loss. We now know the exact pharmaceutical formula for black mollies. This formula that produced diet pills in the '60s is known today as methamphetamines and is a worldwide killer, especially in America.

The methamphetamine epidemic now permeates every small town and large city in America. It is also a fact that meth users run in packs like wild dogs, enhancing their creativity and ambition to do evil. It creates such a strange behavior in its users that it creates a proclivity that can lead to murder—even the murder of the user's parents in some cases. What starts out as an energy boost can put you in the company of demons while using this drug. Its ability to change the flow of good to evil is of supernatural danger.

Thankfully, one characteristic that's prevalent among meth users is the fact that before they can implement their plans, they either run out of money or meth. Also many of the crazy and murderous schemes that materialize while using meth is quelled by a short attention span; then they go on to something else.

If there was ever a drug that can ruin your family name, it is this drug. Meth can put you or your family name on the same level as Charles Manson and his followers; this drug has that capability, and it happens frequently. It creates a temporary physical super-endurance that works in collusion with evil ideas, and can make a once-good kid do things you only hear about in horror stories.

The user is left with a depleted body void of essential minerals such as potassium and magnesium; and of course, all water-soluble vitamins. The loss of vitamins and nutrients can also cause a temporary lack of logic in the mind and will fuel crimes. This drug can literally create a science-fiction zombie apocalypse if enough people use it. It can turn morally balanced and reasonable human beings into everything from pedophiles to individuals who murder for sexual thrills. It can also cause normally decent people to perpetrate crimes for small amounts of money. The crimes that are done while on meth renders the perpetrator guiltless. When the user is shooting this drug (which has become a very popular method), they can easily align themselves with negative energy. This drug can influence a normally sane mind, and can open a Pandora's box of evil that does not exist in the natural dimension.

It is also true that during the 1940s, methamphetamine was used in Germany during World War II; and that Hitler's army marched while on bathtub crank, as it was called. We now know that the term 'blitzkrieg' means 'lightning war'—quickly overwhelming enemy armies with heavy firepower and massive mobile forces (The History Channel). Today, a variant of the German word ('blitz') is used in American professional football.

In the 1960s, we began to embrace a commodity that gave young people a chance to escape without ever leaving. Marijuana has been call the 'gateway drug', but many have challenged this analogy. Whether you think of it as a gateway or not, it is true that it gave its users a chance to escape while they were using it.

Today's medical research uses marijuana to treat the side effects of chemo treatment and cancer. If marijuana is so harmless and safe, then why is it called a gateway drug? The problem came to America in the form of illicit marijuana sales. Know this: the dealer who sells pot today will sell your child heroin or cocaine tomorrow. This illegal sale of marijuana is sold by same drug dealers who are selling heroin and cocaine. These dealers now have access to pharmaceutical fentanyl that can kill your child in one night. Fentanyl can and is used to lace pot, coke and heroin to enhance them and make them more addicting.

America would soon get a revolution in rock and roll, starting with the Beatles. Until this time, Elvis and many like him were the gold standard for America's youth. Along with the Beatles would come dozens of rock-and-roll groups, a rebellious attitude, and open morals.

America's colleges were a flashpoint of insurrection; its students, as a generation, were unhappy with the Vietnam War. Their goals were to expose racial injustices the Vietnam War, and to rebel against the establishment. America's youths were experimental in their thought process, and the results were bad.

Television was coming out of its infancy then. After a hard day's work in the '60s, every American dad could see bullets flying and soldiers dying live, thanks to T.V. This created insurrection and insubordination in our universities; and to be fair, not all of their complaints were wrong.

The hippies and the youth in the '60s weren't completely wrong in their objectives, but were wrong in their solutions. These were the baby boomers who created what would be known as the 'generation gap'. These same baby boomers who embraced drugs as a way of escape have become a very unhealthy generation fifty years later. This generation has access to the world's greatest medical facilities; but have been cursed with the largest percentage of diabetes, high blood pressure, cancer, and (most importantly) heart problems—more than any generation in our history. It appears that 50 years of drug use wasn't conducive to a previously healthy generation. It is also important that you understand that the children who are on meth and heroin now are the children and grandchildren of that generation.

In the '60s, mankind was beginning to see the results of technological benefits that were a side effect of NASA's space race. War and the space race produced technological and medical advantages that ultimately made life better.

NASA was in its prime, and was favored and fueled by our young president, John F. Kennedy. His challenge to America and NASA was to go to the moon, therefore showing the world that American technology could beat the Russians. And it worked: this race to the moon putting America against the giant Soviet Union helped end the Cold War.

When we won the space race, it proved to the entire world that American ingenuity was the best on the planet. This also confirmed that our technology and missile delivery systems in case of nuclear war would probably be the most deadly and efficient.

Enormous breakthroughs because of space-age research produced benefits in the world of physics, science, and medicine that led to nanotechnology and computer-based industries. These industries would serve every human being on the planet. Experiments that were done by NASA in space (in an anti-gravity environment) produced results that are unobtainable on Earth.

I am convinced that even with his personal weaknesses, John F. Kennedy was a enormous benefit to mankind. His charisma united both liberals and conservatives, but someone did not like his plan.

Soon after his death, America would lose another great civil rights leader (Martin Luther King); and then the late president's own brother, Robert Kennedy. It has been said that the good die young. Nothing makes our case more than these three great Americans. These three men's words will make any red-blooded American have goosebumps.

America had about 200 million inhabitants at this point. We have now increased our population by 130 million. However, the rest of the planet has more than tripled our global population, going from three and a half billion to almost eight billion people.

Of course, overpopulation has created new stresses on our planet. It has pushed us closer and closer together, causing a strain on our planet's resources that is really the cause of global warming, epidemics, and the starvation of millions.

Closer living conditions across the world, especially in America, has generated a type of stress that has also facilitated drug use. While more and more industrialized nations (especially China) spew out copious amounts of industrial products, they're creating pollution that circles the globe, giving our planet a bad case of pneumonia. This pollution created in China via our jet stream gives us another China import.

The average American still lives like a king compared to people in many other nations. How long will this last? This affluent lifestyle is the reason why millions want to come here; and they will do this legally or illegally, and at any cost. Many of these immigrants who have invaded our nation brought their drug deals and drug connections with them.

In America, we eat what we want and go where we want. This gives us unparalleled freedom that has never existed in history.

There is nothing wrong with affluence, and I am certainly a proponent of freedom. But if the entire world lived on a scale exactly like America's, we would all be dead from pollution in a year. However, the truth indicates that the rest of the world is approaching a level of materialism similar to ours, and produces like never before.

Marijuana gave the kids of the '60s the ability to escape mentally from this planet and its troubles without having to leave. It doesn't take an economist to realize that no farmer will grow agricultural crops for $60 a bushel when marijuana, cocaine, or poppy plants bring a thousand times more. Farmers in third-world nations and in the Far East realized that mountains of money could be made off the young, naïve, and wealthy kids in America. This cycle of purchasing created a cycle of producing and selling, which has then become a circle of death.

For those of you who would still defend and make the claim that marijuana is not a gateway drug, ask anyone who's lost a loved one. If you do the research and study the obituaries, you will discover that 95% of heroin or coke overdoses were people indoctrinated to drugs by the use of marijuana.

The argument has been made that legalizing drugs and taxing drugs will make drugs less dangerous. As an individual and a writer, I concur that marijuana should be legal for medicinal purposes only.

There are two rules that most addicts will agree with me about:

1. Don't get caught with illegal drugs.

2. Don't get caught doing a crime to get money to buy drugs.

If illegal drugs and narcotics such as heroin were legal, rule number one would not exist. This makes rule number two less important, and would give the user an opportunity to blame our laws for their addiction and crime.

Getting back to marijuana and it's legalization... whether you believe pot leads to stronger substance abuse or not, you must admit that it lowers ambition and productivity. If it's a medicinal or therapeutic herb, if you're not sick, why would you need it? When your child or your loved one loses their ambition and drive to be productive, the pot dealer will sell them heroin meth or coke.

We will soon cover how our factories produced sloppy merchandise in the '70s before drug testing, mostly because of the marijuana epidemic. These substances have a biological and a physiological addiction that marijuana does not have, and produce an entirely different person.

This logic proves we have gone full circle and shown the connection to pot, a gateway drug.

In the '60s, as the drug cartels began to organize and gain structure in Mexico, a new industry was beginning to flourish. Their drug sales would be larger than those of any single corporation in America. They also had no safety standards, no taxes, and no government infrastructure to answer to, except for illegal bribes and payoffs.

The word 'cartel' was used to describe drug dealers south of the border, as well as oil cartels in the Islamic world. Their motives and techniques were quite similar. The number-one purpose was to overcharge and regulate, kill, and destroy the American dream and turn it into the American Tragedy.

America, if you think the oil cartel did not create thousands of deaths in our country, you are wrong. Just as the drug cartel in Mexico was invading and poisoning our youth, the oil cartel realized it could influence American cultures and control it with the sale of oil. These Muslim nations hated us for our Christianity and our ideals for thousands of years. They held their tongue and their actions while we were strong, especially during World War II.

With the sale and the astronomical amounts of cash produced by oil-rich Muslim nations, old animosities that began thousands of years ago resurfaced. These old wounds go all the way back to the holy wars and the great crusades. These animosities were already in the mind of the Islamic world; but prior to the sale of their oil and money from America, China, and Europe, they did not have the means to attack us. Some theologians and scholars will concur that this hatred started in the Old Testament with Ishmael, Isaac and Jacob.

Let's get back to our time machine. In the '60s and '70s, money was the initial and primary motivation for drugs. Mexico had always been a poor and starving nation, but could have acquired wealth without the sale of drugs. It has just as many resources and capabilities as America. Money is the driving force today, coupled with the agenda to incapacitate our entire nation, if possible.

I guess that after writing this book, my vacation will not happen in Acapulco or Cancun. It's not that I wouldn't be welcome, but there's a different problem. These two destinations were once two of the greatest places to visit on your honeymoon, or just on vacation. But in 2019, things are different compared to just ten short years ago; and much more different than in the '70s, '80s, and '90s.

It appears that the old saying "You can't swim in a cesspool and come out smelling like a rose" is true again. The drug cartels have created a cesspool of drugs, murder and mayhem in their own backyards. This is further proof of karma, if that's how you want to look at it. Millions of Americans who have lost loved ones think Mexico deserves this: "Live by the sword, die by the sword."

The same drug cartels that polluted these tourist destinations are the same cartels that have caused millions of deaths on the streets of L.A., Chicago, Dallas, or any other big city in the U.S.

Many people believe that the Mexican government is just a facade, and that the drug cartels are really calling the shots.

One of the benefits of having Donald Trump for a president is his drug policy. No matter how you feel about his personality or style, he has a serious drug policy. The very fact that he is an outsider means he's not on the take as an established politician from the drug lobbyist or cartels. The existing and established politicians are the ones who allowed this to happen to America for the last 60 years. By voting in an outsider, the American public made their intentions known. When we secure our borders and Americans can't buy drugs, our cities will clean themselves up without violence.

Little do the Mexican people realize that this new president will be saving them by the same process. America, if there is no market and if the drugs can't get delivered, these would-be businessman will be forced to go into more legitimate and harmless careers. Of course, this will never happen for as long as drugs find their way to the streets. This process that has occurred for 60 years with drugs and negative energy will slowly begin to reverse. When the drug cartel dies, a cleaner and more prosperous way of life will happen for Mexico. I would also like to interject at this point and say to the Mexican people that the masses are not the evil people who are dealing drugs.

Most hard rockers and entertainers in the '60s were thought of as synonymous with drugs and drug use. These groups made drugs even more appealing to millions of our youth. This is not to indict all rock and rollers during this time; many were good and decent artists.

Starting in the '50s, we knew we could all be annihilated within 30 minutes because of intercontinental ballistic missiles or ICBMs. This danger is just as prevalent today, but it's just not talked about because it robs you of peace of mind as a human being.

Marijuana gave this first generation exposed to this possibility a way of escaping. This era of young people knew that death could materialize within 30 minutes if the wrong person pushed the right button. We were the first generation to have this knowledge, and to realize there was a target on our back. We never knew when it could be pushed.

Our universities and our youth were experimenting with designer drugs, LSD, mescaline, and an entire array of mind-bending drugs now called antidepressants as well as behavioral-control drugs.

Of course, the large drug dealers and the drug cartel were aware that if the rich kids buy pot today, they will buy heroin or coke tomorrow. Their sales, their ideology, and techniques evolved like a manufacturing corporation, but their CEOs were called 'kingpins'.

The third-world cartels' long-term objective was to actually own America. Other nations had the same idea. These Mexican and third-world cartels that materialized in the '60 were selling America oceans of drugs at the same time the Middle East cartels were selling oceans of oil.

Street dealers who come out at night are the foot soldiers in this war, and are like cockroaches. Their objective is to own your child by addiction, and use them until they are dead or in prison forever. Now, street dealers are all across America, on almost every street corner, by the hundreds of thousands. Immigration wasn't such a big factor in the '60s because they only comprised about 4% to 6% of our population. In other words, their numbers were just not that large. But now, their numbers are 20% to 35% of our population, and they sway's policies toward their original countries in their favor.

It is also true that thousands of illegal immigrants are dangerous criminals and drug dealers. This is why immigration should be treated as a different crime, but it is a crime. Illegal immigration is related to the murder of our children and burglary of our nation.

Illegal-immigrant drug dealers should be treated the same as terrorists. After all, their objective is to subvert and kill the American people. If there is a difference, it is because the drug cartel has killed millions compared to a few thousand by terrorists.

It is obvious that the Mexican government has had a long-term vision for America and its workforce: to replace American with Mexican labor. It is also true that the American government and its people were very naïve. It appears that the war that existed 200 years ago, when America defeated the Mexican Army starting at the Alamo and San Jacinto, isn't really over. As you can see, we are now losing our national sovereignty through immigration and drug dealers.

Let's get back in our time machine and go up to the 1970s. For those of you old enough to remember, in the '70s, there were gas lines as far as the eye could see due to the oil embargo.

The Arab states caught America off-guard. We had settled into our role of producing 8,000-pound automobiles. These dinosaur cars had the average gas mileage of 11 or 12 miles per gallon. We were locked in to these gas hogs, and were reliant upon Middle Eastern nations to keep them running. Many of our plants and the automobile industry produced shoddy cars, many which had a lifespan of only 70 or 80 thousand miles. After admitting this problem, and with competition coming in from Asia, we are now producing automobiles with double that mileage.

It is common knowledge that marijuana was one of the contributing factors for the production of poor-quality automobiles. Almost all of the cars produced in the '70s and '80s are the scrap iron used today to build bridges and highways.

It is also a characteristic of pot smokers that generates the 'whatever, I don't care' laid-back attitude in the workforce. These marijuana users in the '70s and '80s that number into the tens of millions weren't using pot for medical reasons; they were escaping.

By the '70s, the pot smokers were not escaping the fear of ballistic missiles or a nuclear war. They were simply escaping their responsibilities. When the legalization of marijuana is debated and considered, this attitude should always be remembered..

There are some who will argue that if we accept marijuana because it's a herb or a plant, then why not the poppy seed or the coca leaf, which produce heroin and cocaine?

In the '70s, not only were the Mexican drug cartels and the Middle Eastern nations seizing this opportunity and this moment of weakness, but so were China, Japan, and most Asian nations. I believe Richard Nixon had good intentions, but his visit to China awoke a sleeping giant that could outproduce anyone in the world. He unleashed a nation that had a willing and very large population that worked cheaper than even Mexico, and would soon be a world superpower.

Not only were the Japanese and Chinese engineers prepared to produce better-quality and more fuel-efficient cars, they would work for one-third of what an American worker would accept. There still isn't parity, but we are getting closer and closer to working for the same wages; and eventually, for less.

At the close of the '50s, America was producing the greatest automobiles and products on the planet. For two decades after World War II, America held all the cards. It was no coincidence that poor workmanship materialized side by side with the introduction of drugs in America for the masses.

Now that we have the first real president to take on this fight with sincerity, he is strangely being attacked domestically by the so-called free press. His attempt to do good for the American people while under attack by fake news is no coincidence.

Nations that are our enemies love it when our media's false narratives try to undo a legal election. They also love our drug epidemic.

It is one thing to expect foreign adversaries to try subverting our nation. But this attack by mainstream media is tantamount to treason.

America had become the world's industrial giant by the end of World War II. This produced millions of rich kids in America. Someone once asked Clyde Barrow why he robbed banks. Clyde replied, "Because that's where the money is." He may not have been an honest man; but you have to admit, that was an honest answer.

This is also true of the drug cartel and why they sell us drugs, and why the Middle Eastern nations sell us oil: we are where the money's at. The Islamic people have an ambivalent love-hate relationship with America; but for the most part, it is secret hate. They love our money, the products we produce, our agricultural goods and technology. They just hate the American people.

Of course, for those who will tell the truth and are not afraid of political correctness, the real beef that they have with America is our Christianity and our commitment to Israel. During the Obama Administration, the term 'Islamic extremist' was forbidden for fear of offending Muslims. This same political correctness that tied a ball and chain around America didn't affect Islamic extremists, or stop them from beheading Americans on live T.V. while he was president. Prior to Mr. Trump, we in America had been acclimated by leaders who told us what we wanted to hear rather than truth.

The drug epidemic of marijuana and cocaine in the '80s was bad enough, but a new super-form of cocaine was about to be unleashed on society. Crack cocaine would be just as addictive to lawyers, bankers, or doctors as it was to blue-collar workers. There was no discrimination in the death and destruction.

Early on, the euphoric high wasn't even understood. It appeared the combination of baking soda and cocaine would create a high that, once smoked, 70% of its users would be instantly addicted to. Crack cocaine would be the largest leap of destruction to ever fall on an affluent society. It destroyed millions of Americans financially, physically, spiritually and emotionally. The higher up in society you were, the further you would fall.

This epidemic of crack cocaine that started in the '80s and '90s is still occurring, and hasn't been matched in destruction. Even a full-scale war could not have done more damage to a society as did the crack epidemic. Crack was responsible for more deaths in the '90s than all other drugs combined. It is now taking a backseat to heroin and pharmaceutical drugs.

Most who have used crack or meth will tell you that they're lucky to be alive today. One thing addicts have in common is if they survived either crack or meth, it wasn't by their own choice. Yes, I'm talking about jail. Law enforcement sometimes have a way of saving us, whether we like it or not.

Methamphetamine is a drug favored and used by blue-collar and less affluent white middle-class people. Meth has been called the 'poor white man's cocaine'. Tens of thousands of blue collar everyday Joes and Janes of most lower to middle class communities became addicted to meth because of its fake energy. Others in high-pressure professions were also vulnerable; many have subsequently died or suffered from strokes.

If they were lucky, these salespeople went to jail first. Getting a jail sentence separates the user from the drug and his acquaintances. This time in jail also puts time and distance between them, their addiction, and the dealers.

One characteristic concerning methamphetamine users is geography. When you remove them from the neighborhood, the town, and the state where they committed their crimes, there is a 70% chance of recovery after rehab and probation. It takes time for the user in a new town to make connections and to generate enough trust to re-enter this circle of methamphetamine death. Meth dealers know the consequences, and they are cautious. The encouragement and reinforcement to not return to meth should be pushed and monitored by rehabs if their clients are released on probation.

Meth has changed the character of America in a negative way. The bravery and patriotism that was a part of the Americans during World War II diminished in the '60s. Our democracy and capitalism that made us the most affluent nation on Earth is under attack.

Chapter 3

A Nation of Addicts

One thing that frightens people while they're on an airplane, a fast boat, or any other method of transportation is their lack of control. We like to be in control of every second and moment of our lives. We don't trust anyone as much as we trust ourselves. In most cases, we are better off with someone else doing the job. If it's flying an airplane, operating on our gallbladder, or representing us in a criminal case, we have no control.

Fortunately, almost 99.9% of the time, if you use mass transit, you'd arrive safely and probably more so than if you were driving.

There is one affliction that can harm and kill you, but you have no control over it. If this happens to you or someone you love, it will be many times worse; and will last longer than a 3-hour flight from Dallas to Vegas. Instead of your ability to hire a good attorney, doctor, or airline pilot to do the professional work for you, there is no one in this field to comfort, guide you, and get you from point A to point B safely. When you get a phone call from the hospital or jail about one of your children in the A.M. hours, it could be the beginning of sorrows.

Often, they have been arrested for drug paraphernalia, or a crime committed while on drugs. Many are arrested with drugs on them. If so, you have just entered a time of trouble that you will have no control over.

There is no infrastructure to guide a parent, or anyone else with a professional title who can help you. Parents who do consult professionals and rehabs discover that their love is exploited by people in the medical field. This medical industry quite often causes the addiction; if the word 'circle' comes to mind, that is exactly what it is: a circle of death motivated by money. Yes, there's an entire industry built around this problem that you will eventually consult.

After months or years of stress, pain, and worry, you might or might not save your loved one. There is no mental, emotional, or financial assistance for you, the parent, or for someone who has fallen into addiction. Many turn to religious leaders for consultation or prayer in the hopes that God will intervene; and sometimes, he does.

It is harder to regain control of and discipline a child once they have become addicted to drugs than it would be for you to actually go up to the cockpit and fly that airplane yourself. You will no longer be dealing with a person who respects your opinion, or a person who has the same logic and cooperation that could solve other medical problems.

If your child is in their 20s, 30s, or even a teenager, you are still in uncharted waters. This is not a biological disease at first; this is a mental hijacking. The frustration that you will experience will generate anxiety upon you, and will create a feeling of not having control.

But it will get worse. The person you nurtured and raised has been exposed to something worse than most diseases. Most of us who are good parents initially decide to take this on without ever considering that we might lose. That just isn't a part of our thought process or mindset at this time.

If you think the aforementioned 3-hour flight from Dallas was scary and you wish you had more control, you ain't seen nothing yet. This new battle for control could take weeks or years, with death as the usual outcome.

Most parents start out with this attitude: they are going to take control, defeat this problem, and save their child; no force on this planet can stop them. This changes after about a year. It's not that the parents give up or quit trying; it's just that the struggle, stress, emotional drain and financial costs put them in more danger than the drug user. In some cases, the addiction and the personality of the child is so extreme, the only thing a parent can do is literally follow that child into the grave.

The type of fight that you will be in to regain control and save your child's life will depend upon the kind of drug they have been using. Once you get to this point, instead of getting your child out of jail, you are thankful they've been incarcerated—it allows you a few days of rest until they go in front of the judge and are usually released. In some cases, judges will require court-ordered rehab, which is a great thing.

If your child isn't caught up in many cases, you, the parent, will try to have them arrested out of desperation. Your fight is against time, money, and energy; but you're older by now and don't have these things. Also, these drug dealers have embraced a type of evil that you can't quite get your mind around. It appears that evil and violence are their mantra, their code of conduct; and these permeate their personalities as they align themselves with evil entities.

While you are fighting to get your child off of heroin or some other drug, that child can be exposed to other powerful drugs that can kill in one night. Yes, when your child is on heroin and they discover opiates, morphine, Demerol or other opioids, there is a chance they will experiment.

There is a new and modern powerful drug called fentanyl. This drug is 700 times more powerful than heroin. If your child injects this opioid without knowing about its dangers, they can be dead in minutes. Fentanyl use is growing exponentially all across America, and it is mixed into other more benign drugs (like marijuana) to enhance their addictive quality and capabilities. This is done secretly, and the user isn't aware of its presence quite often until it's too late. And some drug dealers are committing murderous acts with fentanyl for kicks.

These are the types of scenarios that you are about to experience—and must resist. This is a real hell on Planet Earth that you never thought existed. This hell is designed to steal your loved ones, their money, and your sanity; and will ultimately kill both of you.

Fentanyl is not the only one that can kill your child overnight, but it is the most prevalent and recent killer. On one occasion, it killed as many as 11 people in one county overnight. Unlike an airline flight or anything else in modern transportation, this will be one flight you cannot cancel because it wasn't you who bought the ticket.

Within the last 40 years, millions of parents across America have had that 3 A.M. phone call. We don't believe it could happen to us; we think we had educated our child correctly and it only happens to other people. We now know this isn't the case, and thinking it can't happen to us is very dangerous.

Unfortunately, in America, there is a heroin epidemic that drug dealers and third-world countries have found to be very profitable. Once you are addicted to heroin, you rarely turn back. If you try to get clean, these dealers pursue you for the sale. You don't have to hunt them down because you are now a cash cow.

At that point, if you're the parent, your life is about to change in a way you never imagined. After this fight, a plane crash may look like a better outcome for your life. This is why you must be armed with knowledge. After you know the truth, which has been obscured and hidden for a variety of dangerous reasons, you have a head start.

The best way to defeat opiate or heroin use is prevention. Unlike cancer or heart disease, there is an 100% sure way for America to defeat this problem: to prevent availability. I will talk more about this later.

Before we get to the real substance of this chapter, please allow me to make a real-life observation. If no one in your family is on drugs or has ever been on drugs, you are blessed; but you're a rare minority. We seem to have a zombie apocalypse or science-fiction thriller on our streets, and the consequences to the American population are similar. When you go to the theater, go shopping, or take your child to school, there is a 100% chance you are surrounded by people whose minds are being controlled by narcotics. In essence, we are a zombie-like population.

We know that texting is dangerous while you drive, but there is even more danger in drug use than texting while driving. You won't see them turn up a can of beer or wobble, but millions are on the highway popping pills. These drivers don't usually get ticketed or recognized as being high if they're pulled over. That's because most of them have been taking opiates so long, the average cop doesn't recognize the high. 30% of the drivers on our roadways are high on pain pills, Xanax, Valium or other pharmaceutical drugs.

Most of these pain-pill users are not criminals, but they are everywhere and permeate every segment of society by the millions. The truth is that 95% of Americans have been involved either as a victim of drug-related crimes or even worse; 26% have been the perpetrator of a drug-related crime. These may be conservative figures by some estimates, and it may be as high as 60%. The crimes range from very petty (for example, stealing your identity) to much, much worse.

Many more violent crimes and atrocities are committed every day. Turn on your T.V. and watch the news, and notice the drug connection. There are shootings and deaths in big cities like Chicago, Detroit, L.A., Oakland, Houston, or Philadelphia by the hundreds. Most of our cities are more dangerous than the front lines of Afghanistan.

There was a time in America when the wealthier could move to the affluent suburbs to escape drug and criminal activity. We now know this is not true, and the drug dealers have followed the money; the crimes follow the dealers. They range from murder, robberies, or any and every crime that can be conceived of in the human mind to procure drugs or to support a lifestyle. This is an absolute fact, and you can check the statistics. There have been more Americans murdered and killed as a result of drug-use—either directly or indirectly—in the last 60 years compared to those who have died in all our wars combined.

Before you finish reading this chapter and before you can put down this book, know that several Americans across the US have been murdered because of drugs while you were reading. Millions of smaller crimes caused by drugs would have been committed before this chapter ends. In fact, if you're not in a safe place, you should look over your shoulder.

Most of these crimes are perpetrated in the quest to acquire more drugs. It would take an astronomical figure to itemize all of the types of drugs and crimes, but they are in the millions. However, most shootings are done by gang members or drug dealers over turf wars and retribution.

Keep in mind the person you raised, took to Sunday school, and explained right from wrong to is no longer controlled by sound logic. Our penitentiary and judicial fields have millions of cases with crimes that do not fit the person. Some of these crimes are so bizarre that many perpetrators would think nothing about murdering the very people who love them. This is the reality, the shock, the horror that many parents are waking up to after finding out that their loved ones have stolen their money and belongings.

After some of these users rob their parents, employers or friends, they rush to the nearest drug dealer. These drug dealers are the cockroaches of human society: they come out at night as soon as the lights and the exposure is gone. They are the lowest of the low among humans.

It takes one nation to poison and addict another. The most important player in close proximity to the United States, I'm sorry to say, is none other than Mexico. It is not the only one that procures and then delivers death and destruction to our youth, but it is the closest. This epidemic has been occurring across our borders in enormous quantities now for 70 years, with all kinds of political excuses and promises to allow it to continue.

The Mexican authorities and Mexican drug dealers' argument goes like this: If there wasn't a market in America for these drugs, there would be no one to fill that market. Unfortunately, that is true. But this explanation does not exonerate Mexico. In fact, it indicts them more than ever in my opinion because this is an actual admission of guilt. It is also true that Mexico has cultivated this addicted culture in America.

We are going to be honest in this book and not politically correct, just correct. This necessitates telling the truth. As a writer, I have no other intentions at any cost. But after all, the truth is that they've already killed millions of us; what else can they do?

I am not blaming only Mexico. The Mexican drug cartel and government are well aware of the deaths, with no remorse and no apologies. I say this without reservation because if they had any conscience, it would stop.

It is a fact that Mexico has addicted more Americans than any other country on Planet Earth. Of course, this is because of its proximity to us. And now, some 70 years since the drug war began, more than 40% of our population are involved with drugs in one way or another.

Now that 30% of our workforce cannot pass a drug test and are a danger to themselves and their employer, guess who sent in its own workforce? You got it: Mexico. Mexico was planning not just 5 years or 10 years ahead, but 50 years. It appears that its strategy was long-term to incapacitate much of the American workforce with drugs. After this, Mexico would replace those American workers with Mexican immigrants.

This thought process occurred to a population and a government with time on their hands and nothing to lose. It doesn't take a NASA engineer, rocket scientist, Albert Einstein, or a think tank to spell 'conspiracy'. Our leaders, some of our legislators, and many other large corporations are a part of this conspiracy, either willingly or unwittingly.

It should also be mentioned that hundreds of thousands of employers, especially in construction, have capitalized on illegal workers. Many of these contractors would have never been successful without illegal immigration. The biggest reason why American contractors hired them is because illegals are willing to work for half the usual price. It is also true that these employers and contractors, in some cases, had no choice because the average American is incapacitated on drugs.

Unlike many other natural or biological calamities that have been perpetrated, with this one, you can follow the money. Our new president has changed the North American Free Trade Agreement (NAFTA) and called it what it really was: another way of smuggling drugs.

Let me be very adamant, and reiterate once again that this does not exonerate Americans for their drug use in any way. To allow Mexico to disable the American workforce with narcotics and then send in their own workforce was a double betrayal. Mexico is known for certain types of drugs, such as cocaine, marijuana, and a much stronger form of methamphetamine. Meth is produced all across America, but isn't as powerful.

While Mexico is not known for the production of heroin, it is the vehicle and the trajectory route that many countries such as Afghanistan have chosen to deliver to your child. There has been an apparent effort by our legislators to allow drugs to cross our southern border. It is obvious that some of our very top leaders, and I do mean top, have allowed drugs to cross our southern border. One has to ask: Have some of these leaders received large amounts of cash under the table?

The leaders from other countries that hate us are also watching our borders and see what the drug cartel has accomplished, creating a model that they will use. These leaders and their scandals steal billions and cut bad deals, but nothing on Earth is as bad and tragic as the millions of deaths in the drug war.

During the Clinton administration, there were many articles, books and accusations pointing to drug deals in Arkansas while Bill Clinton was still governor. It is alleged that planes full of drugs were allowed to touch down in Arkansas, with no interdiction, confiscation or prosecution. If I make the Clinton investigations a part of my book, I am afraid I won't do my job to warn you as a parent because that would be a book in and of itself.

These open borders have also been a gateway in the past 20 years that could have delivered a nuclear suitcase, bomb or some other biological weapon that could kill tens of thousands or millions. It is no secret to the Islamic world or terrorists that our borders are open; and if you want to cross over, you seem to have some of our leaders' blessing.

This entire outlook on drugs has been to prosecute and indict the American people for something that could have been stopped at the borders, but was allowed to continue. This way of thinking has created an entire industry in our nation that is based on the lack of security, lawlessness, death and destruction. Security is just one small part of the results. In our nation, almost all jails, courts, rehabs, probation facilities, attorneys, bondsmen and bounty hunters owe their jobs and fortunes to the drug epidemic.

Drug dealers will not like this chapter; they will not like its exposure. Their sinister and demonic motives will allow you to see this from the eyes of a seasoned expert. The subject matter gets more adult and more serious as we go along: drug sales and the drug underworld are also very connected to sex trafficking and human slavery. Yes, if your child is a slave to heroin or any other drug while on the streets, they are vulnerable to sex trafficking or white slavery. In all fairness, I think it's an indiscriminate slavery of all races for money.

Most Americans would never perpetuate or be a part of these crimes prior to their addiction. Once a person goes so far and so deep into the drug culture, the first thing that is disarmed is their conscience. Our conscience works much like an altimeter on an airplane that keeps us level and informs us, but it's incapacitated by the use of long-term drugs.

Drug dealers do not like our new president Donald Trump because he is the first leader to really take this problem on with no fear. His analogy of draining a swamp appeared elementary to me at first, but I now realize how accurate it was and is.

Just as we are getting our minds wrapped around the drugs that cross our borders and how they decimated our nation, we now have a new and much closer domestic threat. This new enemy, of course, is the giant pharmaceutical industry.

There is absolutely a toss-up today as to which of these enemies are killing more of our children. For many years, pharmaceutical drugs were considered safe and harmless because Americans believed that if a doctor prescribed it, we should be okay with it. We now know that if we follow the money, just as many are dying from pharmaceuticals than street drugs. Shockingly, we now know that doctors are the top stockholders in the giant pharmaceutical industry.

Please do not misunderstand me. Let's stop immediately, and let me make one thing clear: not all doctors are overprescribing. Many doctors are very discreet. Look for signs of abuse. Others, of course, do not care.

It now appears that there is a pill, a liquid, a spray, a powder, or an injection for almost every ailment that has ever plagued mankind. Doctors are the new dealers and pushers, but have now taken the street dealers' place. They have joined them in a rather unholy union to compete for the money.

This means we are being attacked at home and on the street. It's well-known fact, and many school children who are now on black tar heroin will tell you that their addiction started from Mama and Papa's medicine cabinet.

The top prescriptions written by almost all doctors are for hydrocodone, Percocet, oxycodone, and so many more that are based on synthetic opiates. No matter what ails us, almost every doctor in America will quickly reach for his prescription pad to write up these opiates.

Why are they writing up so many prescriptions for pain medication? It's simple: because opiates are very addicting. Once you are addicted, you are guaranteed to visit that doctor's office on a weekly or monthly basis, which would surely increase sales. Yes, doctors are the new drug pushers—some, inadvertently; others, for profit.

Finally when the problem is called out or if the doctor cuts the patient off, that patient (especially a young person) is likely to turn to street heroin. When the pharmaceutical epidemic of pain pills and all types of opiate-based drugs are stopped, heroin dealers will emerge like maggots to fill the orders.

America, know this: the opiates in heroin are the same as the opiates in hydrocodone. The only difference is that one is organic, and the other is synthetic.

If the pharmaceutical industry is forced to cut back on synthetic pain pills, this will be good news for the Golden Triangle. This Golden Triangle is a part of Cambodia, Laos, and Vietnam that sends much of the world's heroin abroad. Its objectives are not just monetary. Like China and other world powers, these nations realize that poisoning and addicting our people is stronger than a military attack. The difference in this attack is that they make billions in profit instead of buying weapons. There have been no shots fired, no country to attack, no leader to blame or grab credit for killing millions of Americans. The poppy plants are indigenous to their region, and are cultivated vigorously with one target and one customer in mind: the USA and your children.

The first attack from the Golden Triangle was during the Vietnam War. Heroin use was rampant among our soldiers in the Vietnam era, with the heroin furnished by the Golden Triangle. Thousands of American soldiers came back to the States with a heroin addiction. The same region is still producing heroin, but it has now reached our streets.

This new addiction that we have because of an innocent trip to the doctor's office has changed our lives for the worse. Heroin dealers know and realize that America's pharmaceutical industry is creating future customers for them. America's death by drugs and our acceptance of death have been slowly perpetrated on us with purpose. We didn't get the wake-up call like we did on 9/11 or Pearl Harbor to instantly unite us. America must realize that drug cartels and third-world countries have used this slow but sure acclimation to addict America. This slow acclimation works the same for pot, methamphetamines, crack cocaine, and any and all pharmaceutical prescriptions.

Synthetic opiates are now mass-produced by the pharmaceutical industry. When the effects of cocaine and opiates were first used in soft drinks like Coca-Cola or Bayer aspirin in the early 1900s, we got our first taste of deception. Mothers were using heroin and didn't even know it until the death rates began to soar. What husbands noticed were their wives' demureness, complacency and cooperative attitude due to opiates. The same attitudes of cooperation, carelessness, and easygoingness are also present in today's population of pain-pill users. Of course, Xanax and Valium weren't available then, but other drugs during this moment in time would be their forerunner: an entire list of other anxiety drugs called diazepams.

This combination of opiates, alcohol, and benzodiazepines (benzos) have killed hundreds of thousands in the last 50 years without much publicity. Ask anyone addicted to opiates or benzos such as Valium or Xanax, and they will tell you that even Xanax is more dangerous to detox from than heroin.

I want to interject and place a thought inside your head: We are all the same biologically. We don't all look the same, but none of us are immune because we are Superman or we live in a nicer home, have more money, or are more intelligent or better lovers. This addiction doesn't care about your race or IQ, or how much you love yourself or your wife; it only wants your life.

No matter how we become addicted, the common threads we all share are exposure and availability. One might make the argument that in some ways, this makes a solution easier to make. It would be if we were all on the same page, but we're not.

Believe it or not, sometimes (more often than not), the lower your IQ, the better your chances are of not doing drugs. This is because unlike the brazen intellectuals who believe they are impervious to danger, you realize and know you're not smart. You know you're not disciplined and know your limits are not enough to handle drugs; and that, my friend, is genetic intelligence or luck.

Many addicts resort to spiritual and emotional help from the clergy. All of these variables eventually come to play in the cure.

like your car, we do have a Check Engine light or a warning light in our bodies to tell us we're doing something wrong. One might argue that just by looking at our bodies and seeing the disintegration, the age, and the stress on our faces, we would change.

By this point, we are deeply involved in the drug culture; and outsiders must intervene because our internal reasoning has been incapacitated by drugs and drug dealers. We say many times that we are going to save ourselves and that we have to do this on our own, but the reality is that rarely works. This doesn't work for the same reason a drowning man rarely saves himself.

It seemed that the pharmaceutical and medical industries have a drug to treat any ailment or infectious disease. If you notice that over half of the commercials that you encounter while watching T.V. are all about pharmaceuticals and medicine, the reason for it is simple. No one else can afford that much air time; and if the air time goes to the highest bidder, no one can compete with these financial giants. If you listen closely toward the end of these commercials for newly released drugs, you'll hear that their side effects range from slight headaches, insomnia, and anything from an itch on your nose to death itself.

Healthcare in America costs trillions of dollars each year; one-third of that is for drugs. It's obvious that we are saturated; and we believe there's a drug for everything, including happiness, sadness, and obesity. Sexual dysfunction is the most important moneymaker. This isn't to forget street drugs; it is only to expose an additional problem.

Xanax has been the top pharmaceutical drug to kill many famous people in the last 30 years, and is becoming notorious. But even Xanax would soon take a back seat to a drug we mentioned earlier: fentanyl. It has the capacity to kill all of us if we were to use it.

As I close this chapter, I would like to say that instead of fighting drugs, the medical and pharmaceutical industry decided they wanted their part of the cash. Americans have all felt the consequences of being lured, attacked, seduced and sedated by both of these drug dealers. The financial difference between street drugs versus pharmaceuticals is that one influences the stock market.

There are scriptures in the Bible that implies that in the last days, you won't be able to find a workman because of drugs. I recently visited someone in jail. While I was there, I couldn't help but notice the demographics of the prisoners. I noticed that most were young, healthy, strong white men; and that they reflected the balance or percentage ratio of white men in my town. I also noticed the same percentage of black prisoners and the population of my hometown. What I didn't see were Hispanic or Mexican prisoners who did not match the demographics or the percentage of Hispanics in our town.

On my way back from jail, I saw something that made sense later. I stopped at McDonald's to get coffee; and I noticed several pickup trucks with construction equipment in the back, among them wheelbarrows and shovels. I then realized and remembered that the workers were all Mexicans, of course.

You don't have to take my word for this. You can check out any construction site; get up in the morning, and look and see who's going to work in the construction industry. Now, you will see 90% Hispanic, 20% white, and 2% black. This is a symptom and a consequence of both pharmaceutical and illicit street drugs. There is an imbalance playing out all across America, and is a strategy by Mexican and other South American governments.

This incapacitation of young, strong, and healthy white males also happens to young, strong, and healthy black males. Millions are either in custody, or on parole or probation and awaiting trial. 95% of the time, their cases are drug-related.

Mexico isn't alone; it's now Chinese and other Asian countries that dominate all electronic jobs. The Chinese and others want us to be consumers, not producers. What better way to do that than drugs? Heroin (most of which comes from Asian countries and Afghanistan) is also used to incapacitate our nation. These drugs are delivered to the docks inside huge container ships.

I am not excusing bad behavior on the part of white or black males; I am only trying to get you to see a different side of this epidemic. If you think for one second that these young people understood this as a motive, you are wrong. They realize that drug dealers have one motive (money), but the governments that protect drug cartels have a different motive (the subversion of America). These leaders desire to take over through globalization; that's their ultimate goal.

I'm not talking about just trade; I'm talking about trade, then reduction in production and a disintegration of military capabilities, after which we will be infected by drugs, even in the military. Yes, even generals and commanders in strategic positions in our military have been tainted and poisoned by the synthetic pharmaceutical opioids pushed by the Chinese. This is not a negative statement about our military because it is the greatest to have ever existed in history; it is only to show that they are also human also.

Remember, the one thing we all have in common is that we are all biological and prone to the same physical weaknesses.

The Chinese, the Russians, and many other countries that are in bed together have one common cause: overthrow America. The reason why we emerged from World War II as the only superpower was because we were the best equipped, the best trained, and the most patriotic and unaddicted military to have ever existed. Let this be understood: if we would have been intoxicated by the drug epidemic during World War II, we would have lost that war.

Chapter 4

The Results on Our Nation

Someone died on August 16th, 1977 in Memphis, Tennessee. That person was Elvis Aaron Presley.

How can opiates—especially prescribed pharmaceutical drugs that are supposed to make life better—take your life? It would be much later after Elvis' death that we would find out for sure that there were too many prescribed drugs involved.

This greatest entertainer to have ever lived came to personify the best that could be offered not just to America, but to the entire world. His looks, talent, and stage performance have yet to be duplicated, although thousands have tried. They say in Hollywood that imitation is the purest form of flattery. No other entertainer has had as many tribute artists and very talented individuals who tried to replace Elvis as Elvis did.

Unlike most entertainers who never mention their faith, shy away from it, or deny it because they don't want to muddy the waters and hurt their careers, Elvis never denied his faith. Even more so today, it is unpopular to align yourself with Christian values in Hollywood. It seems that as a star, you will be under attack from Hollywood's elite if you have these values.

I am not saying that Elvis was perfect, and neither would he if he were here. But look at Hollywood then and now. Today's entertainers are deeply passionate about being left-wing liberals, with no tolerance for anyone else's belief system. For the most part, it has morphed into a cesspool of evil Satanic ritualistic servants who have aligned themselves with evil forces. They are militant and aggressive in their political views and are so vile, many are at par with the characters they portray.

This is the difference between the entertainment industry that America enjoyed at the end of World War II and today. This speaks volume about entertainers like Elvis, who said in a Madison Square Garden interview that he preferred to keep his political views to himself. Afterward, he then stated that he was just an entertainer; and that he wasn't against other actors speaking their views.

To use your notoriety and star power to sway political policies or condemn those who are different is a form of lobbying, and Elvis was right: they are just entertainers. There isn't anything wrong with expressing your political views as long as you know you're right and you don't deny others their equal rights. You could influence millions in the wrong way.

In the last few years, there has been proof that indicts some entertainers as being pedophiles, rapists and sexual deviants. Many of these new Hollywood elites show that their off-stage character eliminates them from good judgment. Actors, singers, and even sports heroes who have never confessed a commitment toward Biblical teachings shouldn't be disappointed in the Hollywood we have today. It is true that occasionally, one stands up for Christian values. But at that point, they are likely to be blackballed from Hollywood or America's sports arenas.

On the other hand, Elvis integrated his gospel music into his performances and his career. I am using Elvis as a reference point not only because I'm a fan, but also because of his charity. The Smithsonian Institute named him the most influential entertainer in American culture for the whole 20th century. No other human being, sports star, entertainer, politician, or even Nobel Prize winner has influenced America more than Elvis. And when he was called on to serve his country, he put his career on hold without reservation; and reported to Uncle Sam immediately.

He was very adamant in his belief in God when he spoke. He also backed up his words with a charitable heart that has been documented by thousands. Elvis didn't wear he belief or religion on his sleeve to impress anyone, but was adamant when questioned about it. He made it clear that while he was called The King, there was only one king; and that was Jesus Christ. He respected others with different beliefs, and that is why he was right.

Along with Elvis's almost-supernatural voice, looks, and talent came America's desire for exactly what he had. This catapulted Presley to the top of the world in the entertainment industry. He set the bar so high that no one would ever reach it again. He may have truly been the greatest entertainer America was blessed with.

After Elvis came the Beatles, the Rolling Stones, and many other hard-rock groups. Many of these groups endorsed open drug use and Satanism. In other words, some may have sold their souls to the devil. Look behind the scenes of the Beatles' *Sgt. Pepper's Lonely Hearts Club Band* album. You will see that their heroes were people like Aleister Crowley. This was the beginning of the new-age, anti-Christian, do-your-own-thing movement that even fueled the hippies in the '60s.

There would be many other famous singers and groups in the '70s that opened a door of satanic evil in their verses and their performances. The last thing that any of these entertainers would embrace or endorse were Biblical principles. These entertainers through their use of mind-bending drugs had an artificial but effective way of looking into evil.

It should be of no surprise to you, America, or for those of you who still haven't had your minds hijacked that Hollywood has endorsed this spiritual warfare on you, the audience. The drug epidemic has occurred side by side with it, and is the rocket fuel for this movement. I do not think that all of America's current entertainers embrace evil, but they are certainly the majority. This is the direction we are going in. It is the spirit that's leading your children, and these are the people they are idolizing .

Drugs facilitate and grease the wheels to spiritual destruction that your child is absorbing 24/7. Hollywood actors, singers, musicians and anyone else with a lot of notoriety live in a world that is constantly critiqued and criticized. This pressure creates a need in these performers to escape in order to maintain some form of personal privacy and sanity. That is too much stress to bear for anyone without some privacy and time alone just to be imperfect and human.

Because of their skills, talents and looks, actors are expected to look great and be like supernatural deities all the time. This doesn't even include the immense amount of physical energy needed to maintain this false, non-human persona. We expect this image, forgetting that the person is still just as human as we are. Some believe this is the price of fame. This idol worship creates a vanity in the performer that no other person is forced to deal with. It is a natural, physiological and psychological condition to create self-induced vanity when millions admire you.

As fans, we may wish at times that we could trade places. But history has proven that being loved by millions can be hell on Earth. This is the reason why many turn to drugs in this industry. Drugs offer a way to mentally and emotionally escape without ever leaving. Those who resort to these drugs (especially opiates) live in a glossy reality where they can be vulnerable to the forces of evil. This reality is blocked out only while they're under the influence.

In reality, when people fight opiate addiction like Elvis did, and if they never defeat it, they feel as if they have let the world down. The higher you are, the further you fall. Like other normal people, he loved his fans and he felt he let us down.

In my mind, this rules out suicide and is more of a fatal consequence of coping with fame. If you don't grasp anything else about opiates know that when coping with personal losses and fighting addiction at the same time, success is almost impossible. You might defeat one enemy like addiction; but not two at the same time, like the loss of one or more family members or divorce.

No matter how strong the person is intellectually, physically, or emotionally, once you try to wing it from opiates, here's what happens. First of all, remember that opiates generate a glossed-over effect on every problem or scenario in life. That is, opiates gloss over whatever is hurting you (a divorce, the death of close relatives, etc.) and cover up the pain.

In severe cases (for example, when someone loses their entire family in a house fire or car accident), doctors administer opiates because of emotional pain when the loss is that great. America, you can ask any opiate addict what the worst part and long-term pain of trying to defeat this addiction is. They will tell you it's emotional pain. For the first few weeks and months of detox, the realization of your losses will be magnified in your mind hundredfold. This generates a sadness and a remorse that makes the user feel guilty, angry ,with every negative emotion. The sad part is that some do commit suicide—accidentally, and in some cases, deliberately.

Quite often, after years of living on the streets, in jails or hospitals, the user is left with no one but themselves. At this point, the loneliness and the realization that you have estranged yourself from your loved ones and it was all your doing is too much to bear. In many cases, the opiate user has perpetrated crimes even against the people who loved and trusted them the most. Of course, that does not dismiss the physical withdrawals, which leave the user with severe weakness, diarrhea, aching all the way to the bone, blurred vision, and other negative effects. They have no ambition and no zeal, and cry with despair.

Another thing that doctors neglect to inform their patients is that long-term opiate use with pills can settle in your bones and may take months to disperse. Strangely, most opiate users know these physical symptoms will pass and get better because of all the times they have tried and failed before.

The long-term convalescence required to regain your dignity and self-respect depends on how long you've been addicted, and what kind of bad things you did. The most important thing to remember is to forgive yourself, but learn from mistakes. One thing that has to be stressed is there are many roads that lead the user back to this condition, on every street and at every hour of every day. I will talk more about that later.

Sadly, people who die from opiate addiction aren't always remembered for the good things they did. Nothing good can come out of losing someone like Elvis, but it has exposed opiates to America. It didn't have to happen. In my opinion, Elvis died of a broken heart. The opiates only facilitated his actual, physical death. His divorce, failing health, and a book outlining his addiction all were too much for any human to endure. He could have defeated any one, but not all together.

Millions more have experienced the same death for the same reasons as Elvis. These millions who have died just like Elvis were not famous, but were loved just as much by their families and loved ones.

It is time for you, America, to remove the distance between you and the opiate user. Your compassion, understanding and patience are their only hope.

Elvis isn't the only actor, performer or famous person that America has produced to die from a broken heart facilitated by pharmaceutical opiates. There are literally hundreds of famous actors we have lost for this exact same reason. Whatever seems so bad, so incurable, so unsolvable in these famous people's minds is magnified by the very drugs they were using to escape their problems. This again is proof that an affluent society that can produce a place called Hollywood, with an audience as large as America, can expect the loss of those we created.

Certain drugs can bring malevolent spirits that do us harm while under the influence of drugs like meth. We're going to discuss in this chapter why people act the way they do while on drugs.

Changing your thought process is the initial response of drugs and biological changes are secondary, but can happen almost at the same time. For instance, at the moment of injection, a heroin or an opioid user will receive a warm feeling of emotional and physical reassurance. This will occur in the body as well as in the mind; and will run tit for tat and side-by-side with physical, mental, and emotional changes.

Most heroin and opiate users have described the feeling of being under the influence of opiates as the closest thing to the comfort, security and peace of being in their mother's womb. In other words, while under the influence of heroin, Percocet, hydrocodone and even stronger opioids morphine or Demerol, the user doesn't see any problems that can't be put off (and they usually are). This creates a major problem in society.

Of course, taking enough opiates will cause the respiratory system to shut down, which is quite often a process that can cause death. This is the reason for overdoses that start with nodding off. And many times, the voluntary respiratory system will simply cease to function.

Fortunately first responders now include narcan in there toolbox to bring many back from overdose of opiates .

This epidemic is now a pandemic in America and the world that is worse than what even Far Eastern countries have experienced. These countries have had opium wars, starting with the Dutch East India Company and the exportation of these drugs going back to the 10th century. Opium and the byproducts of opiates are quite literally the reason why China has not already conquered and ruled the world.

Pain relief was the original use of opiates until addiction occurs, and then pain is no longer important. Now, modern science has synthetically produced the molecular structure of the poppy plant in the form of pain pills. This makes years of cultivation unnecessary and multiplies production by the millions, leading to more availability.

The pharmaceutical industry did not stop at the production of synthetic opiates. It was also the first to introduce the American masses to synthetic meth. This new methamphetamine, once considered 'bathtub crank', was injected and used by Adolf Hitler; but was in pill form during the '60s and into the '90s. These pills were called 'black mollies', and they promised weight loss and more energy. They did produce both effects, but also many deaths. These black mollies were used in almost every industry. They were used by truck drivers, country singers, actors, and even doctors for decades; but they are now banned because of lawsuits.

The new demon on the block, meth, has been called the 'poor white man's cocaine'. Why? Because it costs a fourth of what cocaine costs, and is produced at home or in makeshift laboratories across America. Meth use exploded in the '70s because pharmaceutical mollies were banned. The same result would happen when pain pills are finally banned; that will triple heroin use.

Americans who are strung out on meth have different behaviors than those on opiates, as we pointed out earlier. Opiate users are demure, easygoing and non-violent—at least until you try to take away their drug. Even though they are not violent, they're also not responsible citizens. However, they do not pose the physical strengths or abilities that methamphetamine users exhibit.

Law enforcement has been forced to become almost superhuman themselves in their physical abilities and training to fight this particular epidemic, and to protect you and themselves. Quite often, in the field, they're dealing with millions of Frankensteins who have superhuman strength and horrible intentions. This feeling of being impervious to danger and oblivious to authority has produced a lost generation of young people.

It must be pointed out that while law enforcement has beefed up its equipment and training, the meth has gotten stronger. Now, it is incumbent upon law enforcement to understand this problem, and not become dangerously complacent or overactive.

It is at this point where the police officer on the street doesn't have time for political correctness when saving your life or his. Law enforcement is not to blame the general population who are using drugs and drug dealers are the blame.. This alienation lies on the laps of drugs, the pharmaceutical industry and the drug cartels that push the drugs onto America's masses.

It is very easy for law enforcement to adapt the attitude that everyone who has dabbled in drugs or has any kind of a drug history are dangerous, evil and a threat to them. This makes a simple traffic stop a possible death sentence for you if you have ever been convicted of a drug charge. When an officer pulls you over, your license plate can give that officer in 20 seconds almost your entire life history and your criminal past. Of course, this may not be the person who was once was a dangerous drug addict; but records can be acquired quickly. While knowing this, they must be careful, protect themselves, and still do their job. Officers must have patience tempered by discipline and a reality that has never been dealt with before . Law enforcement must also be aware that this epidemic is one that affects some of their own. The American public must also broaden its knowledge of how this epidemic has caused callousness and profiling in law enforcement.

This is the dangerous atmosphere that law enforcement operates in. It is easy to see why they are alienated and why they feel threatened. The fault lies with our legislative body, the pharmaceutical industry, and the past five administrations that allowed this epidemic to expand. It is true that the drug epidemic started before Ronald Reagan or Richard Nixon took office, but every president has failed. Nothing short of a nuclear war is more dangerous for the United States than this epidemic. It can incapacitate 40% of our capabilities.

Drugs have overwhelmed the medical field and judiciary process. There has been an attempt to eradicate methamphetamine home labs, forcing the labs to be more creative.

The Mexican cartel saw the need for meth that crosses our borders because it is more powerful than domestic meth. This Mexican meth is more sinister, powerful and addicting, making it more popular. The menu from third-world countries has meth on the front page, along with cocaine, heroin and pharmaceutical drugs. Pharmaceutical pain pills from Mexico are also a part of the illegal and illicit street drugs delivered from Mexico. While Mexico has traditionally been just the vehicle to deliver heroin to America, it has now become a heroin producer as well. The poppy plant is now grown there and thriving in their soil and atmosphere, as it does in Afghanistan.

While Mexico enjoys selling drugs to America, its number of murders, decapitations, kidnappings, extortion and crime in Mexico is the highest in any country on Earth. Acapulco, Cancun and the beautiful gulf around Mexico are no longer tourist destinations. Mexico has reaped these consequences on its own people in an effort to hook and kill your child with drugs.

This karma that has been brought about by the drug cartel and not resisted by the Mexican government will finally result in revolution and the overthrow of this nation. It has set the stage for any world player to step in, much like what happened to Cuba in the '50s for similar reasons. During this period in history, the leader of Cuba, Fulgencio Batista, allowed the same behavior with the sale of drugs, prostitution, and gambling, which was minor compared to Mexico's behavior.

Cocaine is no longer the number-one killer of many Americans because of overdoses. When it does kill, it's because of heart failure and restrictions in blood vessels and blood flow. Heroin shuts down the voluntary respiratory system, and so can synthetic opiates in pain pills.

When the DEA tightens the noose around one drug, the cartels simply change delivery strategies. I am in favor of building a wall on our southern border. I am also of the belief a trip north by the drug cartel to our northern border will increase with more drug deliveries. This is not to say that a wall will not dissuade and slow down some of the drugs; it will, and of course will also prohibit 90% of illegal immigrants from crossing our border.

I'm not saying we shouldn't build a wall. We should, and do it along with other efforts. Entering our northern border would probably even be more profitable for the drug cartel. The reason for this is simple: They are not expected to be doing business there. Therefore, they would be less conspicuous. It would require a long trip at sea, but it will be worth it. By going across our northern border, the cartel will avoid interdiction in most of the cities where infrastructure is in place to capture them.

We must admit that we are dealing with very creative and criminal minds. Not admitting it will be a form of hardheadedness that will allow their success. Much of the drugs that traverse our southern border end up in our northern cities near Canada, anyway—from Detroit, Seattle, New York, or Chicago. This will make their job easier.

I am of the personal belief that we need to be much more fluid along both our borders, and that necessitates mobility. Building a wall and then being complacent is more dangerous than having no wall at all.

We're always hearing about big drug busts at our border, on the high seas, or on a dock. These drug busts are allowed to occur and are publicized to appease and distract us from bigger shipments. Just like our war on terrorism, we must think like these criminals to be more clever than this enemy. This idea of open borders has allowed 40 years of infiltration on a very unsuspecting and naïve population by our leaders.

Crimes committed while on drugs have tainted everyone who's ever had a drug charge. Many will argue that is a just reward, but it will only bog down our judicial field and prevent many from being productive citizens. Those who have had only minor transgressions may never rejoin society as productive people. Much of America has developed an attitude and an indifference toward former drug users: when they die, that they deserved it.

Earlier, we talked about how some young people feel they can experiment briefly with small amounts, never having the intention of dying young. This callous and indifferent attitude toward Americans who died from overdoses or drug-related crime leaves out the part of their life where they were good and decent people prior to their drug use. These people didn't wake up one morning while taking a prescription the doctor gave them and know in advance they would be addicts. No one knows in advance that their genetics has given a propensity to allow addiction.

If you think this logic is wrong, ask yourself why some people become addicted and others don't. We've all heard the term 'compulsive addictive personality'. This is a factor, but it is not the most important one. However, it is the most highly accepted reason for people becoming addicts, according to physicians and rehab centers. I think science will eventually prove that it is more genetic and biological than learned behavior.

Science now knows that there are pre-existing circumstances of genetic DNA that some people inherit and others don't. People who have this genetic propensity to be addicted have no control; and of course, ask any gay person and they will tell you they were born that way. This is true for the same reason we don't understand why sexual selection and behavior is different with some people.

Does this mean that all addictions are caused by a genetic propensity? Absolutely not. But it must be explained as part of the overall solution rather than painting everyone with a broad brush. This is also why some people who break limbs, experience horrible burns, and take morphine for weeks in the hospital become addicts and some walk away unaffected.

Modern science has shown that while the mother carries an unborn child, the wrong nutrition; the wrong lifestyle; alcohol, cigarettes or even stress can produce negative results in a child. It gets much worse: many thousands of child-bearing women are now a part of the methamphetamine and pharmaceutical base of drug users. Many infants are born with an active addiction, but they are innocent and have no idea what it is they're craving.

If this doesn't speak to your conscience, if this doesn't explain the unbelievable horror, it's too late for you. America, if you think street dealers or the drug cartel care about an unborn infant, then go ahead. Put this book down, flip the T.V. back on, watch football a soap opera or anything else that has taken away your reality.

If you are a user, you never know when the person you're smoking a joint with or doing a line of coke with will bash your brains out. Of course, that analogy is predicated on you doing drugs, which will place you in a much more precarious scenario. Today's drugs are more and more chemically altered; the behavior becomes more bizarre compared to that from drugs just 10 years ago.

No drug ever recorded in history seems to have as much effect on logic, violence and perversion as does the methamphetamine epidemic. This drug has permeated every small town and large city, and it has required more law enforcement that still cannot meet the task. The meth epidemic has fueled the rise in gangs such as MS-13 that aspire to be a part of this evil. These gangs murder, pillage, rape, and rob, especially while on meth. This creates the perfect storm, and is the reason they're in a gang to begin with; and often fuels their evil intentions. America, if you think for one second that gangs such as MS-13 would not kill and take over this nation state by state, then you really are naïve.

If you are reading this, know one thing: If you do meth, you are opening up a Pandora's Box in the human brain. This area of the brain was never intended to be open, and you will have no control over it. You don't realize that most frightening part is that you may do something you won't remember or be sure of, and wake up incarcerated. When you do methamphetamine, you may wake up in a jail cell after you finally go to sleep in 3 days with blood on your hands and ruin your family name.

Even if you go on to pay your debt to society and spend the rest of your life incarcerated, the damage will be forever. This demonic drug could cause you be put to death because of the crimes you committed while on it. Is that what you really want? Is that drug worth it? Is this high really worth it? Should I get help before I use again? Ask these questions during a moment where you're not under the influence of meth.

A characteristic that meth users have is that the brain never gets enough time away from the drug to correct its course. Once the user is deep into his addiction, this drug spreads throughout the entire neurological system, requiring weeks to evacuate.

If you are a user and you are reading this, do not forget these words, and do not take them lightly: Your current existence, your future, and maybe your eternity are at stake. More importantly, if you are reading this and you are not a user, you may be the only one who can save your loved one, and possibly prevent murders.

If you have a family member using meth and you do not try to intervene, you'll need a good excuse. We now live in a real world with real problems fueled by drugs and demonic forces. The worst thing good men can do is nothing at all. No other drug is more deadly and no other drug has the ability to change your logic within a short time span as meth. This drug can change you the average good old boy into evil or even worse if that's possible.

If you are reading this and you are into meth, the only hope is that you grab this second to comprehend and change directions. These words that you are reading can only give you the truth; you can't change them, and they're not going to give you 20 dollars or a ride to your dealer.

There is only one thing that all drugs have in common: availability. It is the key word, whether we're talking about illicit drugs that cross our borders or pharmaceutical drugs that are literally pushed onto you as a consumer.

Up to 80% of school shooters are under the influence of either street drugs, pharmaceuticals or a combination of both. There is always a big push by liberals to capitalize on shootings, blame guns and our laws, and disarm us. This is the kind of thinking that placed losers in the drug war; it is not conducive to solving the problem. This blames you, law enforcement and our freedoms instead of drugs, third-world nations and the cartels.

Look at the faces of the shooters. Many are under 18, and you can bet on one thing: They didn't work and make the money required to purchase that weapon. It is at this point that your common sense should tell you that the parents who are the closest to that child and know them the most are responsible.

Yes, the parents are partly responsible for these horrors, but have escaped any blame. This rule applies even if the shooting is done in a school by someone still living at home. As the parent, you should be held accountable and prosecuted at least to some degree if you have allowed this to happen. You are especially to blame if you purchased the gun that he used to commit these horrible murders.

This is also relevant if that child has sneaked drugs from your medicine cabinet. Just as responsible as you are for your dog biting your neighbor, you are many times more responsible for the behavior of that child. This doesn't play out right in America. The entitlement to a computer, a couch and a T.V. with no responsibilities is the profile that you often see.

There are other characteristics that parents should look for. Violent video games are counterproductive to a normal mind, especially that of a young person who is in their developing years. Of course, sometimes watching the news with a malleable mind can be influenced and create this type of monster.

Many of these shooters are smoking weed or doing synthetic drugs; yet when these horrors occur, the parent is always adamant that they did not allow drugs in their home. This may be true, but it doesn't exclude or exonerate the parent's responsibility for what that child does outside of their domain and behind their back.

Look into the shooters' eyes in their mugshots. You will notice there's no one at home. Most of these killers are stoic and unaware of what they have done, and have not allowed it to register in their minds. If you are not more intelligent than your child and you do not know how to look for this, sorry, but you are still responsible. The very fact that these young people appear stoic and disconnected is further proof of a mental, spiritual or drug-related hijacking of the human mind.

America's parents who provide a spoiled atmosphere and no work ethic can expect some form of this outcome. As a parent, you should be able to help form their thought processes; and are partly responsible if the child lives at home. Yes, it is necessary as a parent to actually mold the way your child thinks prior to adulthood, and guide their thought process away from this evil. Even if your child is 40 and you are 70, you should still be available to share wisdom, guidance, and leadership for a better outcome in all of life. If you exonerate yourself, be sure to exhaust all efforts first.

The liberal agenda and the fake news media will not like my explanation because they would walk a mile around the truth just to perpetrate a lie and destroy America's second amendment. This narrative of disarming all Americans is capitalized on because of shootings, and is politicized to remove your gun rights.

Don't be so naïve or so foolish as to think that those in power wouldn't utilize this opportunity. What is their motive? Once again, it goes back to sovereignty, borders and globalization: When you disarm a nation, they are easily taken over. Many believe that Chinese and other globalists are paying for these fake narratives. Ask yourself: Why are they trying to capitalize on and sensationalize this kind of news? The answer is obvious: To disarm a nation is to conquer and subdue it. For every gun that is owned by you, America, only one in a million is involved in a mass shooting. And estimates of gun ownership in our country are into hundreds of millions.

The rhyme, the reason, and the numbers are different when you understand that 70% of the shooters are involved with drugs, usually psychotic and doctor-prescribed. Now, we've already explained that all drugs are somewhat psychotic. Foreign governments, globalists, large corporations, left-wing liberals, and fake media all want to take our firearms. But why?

If you don't like this logic or any of these explanations, it only leaves evil supernatural spirits that are also drug-related. What better statement can an evil spirit make while affecting the human mind than to create mass shootings and murder? Watching violent internet videos while using certain drugs are very effective in perverting young minds that are capable of mass shootings. I find it strange that liberals never call for or demand the removal of this demonic mind-bending influence on our children like they do guns.

There is also the possibility of hypnosis paired with pharmaceutical or street drugs that can create a mindset capable of mass shootings. If you don't believe this, then I've got some swampland in Louisiana I'd like for you to look at. The CIA and other foreign players have used drugs and hypnosis for decades to bring about world changes. To be so small-minded and narrow in your thinking that these techniques aren't possibly connected to some shootings makes us naïve. I also find it all strange and suspicious that these same liberals who want our guns are in bed with a giant globalist on a worldwide scale.

We know gun control is just one of several issues that diametrically divide the United States of America. The left is as far left as they can get and the right is as far right as possible, creating negative energy in the middle that pushes both sides further away. If America is to survive and this divide isn't bridged with logic, intelligence, and a love for country, the end is near. You'll soon have no freedom to turn on fake news or to read this book or any other book if they have success.

A stronger work ethic and better-quality products are predicated on Biblical principles, and won't produce a school shooter. Without the fundamental knowledge provided in the Holy Bible, man does not have a blueprint nor the desire to respect each other's opinion. Without this fundamental dimension, it is impossible to move forward and create a better world for all of us. Access to Biblical principles is no longer available to our youth in our universities because of political correctness and liberal thinking. This will allow man's own thinking and logic to dominate his reasoning, and the outcome throughout history has been tragic.

This is the reason I have aligned with a conservative view: because the Democratic party, which I was a part of as a younger man, has changed. What was once full of compassion, logic and patriotism was equally as good for America. The left as we know it today is very persuasive in our universities, medical industry, and political division in every category of life. Aligned with fake media under the cover of political correctness, they are very effective in stopping any American connection to Biblical principles.

Throughout history, no matter what man attempted when he tried to stand on his own and when he didn't base any of his decisions on Biblical principles, it always turned out wrong.

Look at our entertainment industry. Watch any T.V. sitcom or movie made 30 years ago, and compare it to today's work. You will find that there was always a moral lesson with a decent ending in the film industry that is considered heresy today.

When America's founders created our currency and constitution, it always credited God. When America decides that we only trust the dollar bill and not the words of God, we are going backward.

Chapter 5

Drugs, the Brain, and the Mind

It has been said that outer space is the final frontier. Some people also believe that the depth of the ocean still needs to be explored.

One frontier that is much closer, more mysterious, and more powerful than any of these places is the human mind. Yes, this greatest force or frontier has never been mapped; and it shows the potential to be as vast and intriguing as outer space. You can put any label you want on your mind, but it is a force. This entity makes your decisions about everything. In other words, your mind makes up your mind.

Astrophysicists, psychiatrists, spiritualists or everyone who has a title in modern thinking or science will concur that everything we encounter is energy. Energy is how you express love or hate. Whether you're making love, giving flowers, or trying to kill with anger, it's energy. The word 'effort' is a result, and is connected with energy on every level of human logic. You can never leave out this word. We use the word 'energy' when paying our electric bill or buying gas at the pump. We are also programmed to think about energy or how to save it because it is money.

If you are talking about physiological, paranormal, or any other force, either natural or supernatural and you believe it exists, it is energy in one form or another. Don't narrow or limit other dimensions that may be spiritually capable of using energy more efficiently than we can ever imagine.

One night, while we were having a couple of drinks, one of the most intelligent people I've ever known asked me a question. Although I thought I was intelligent, I had no answer. The question was: Could I defy the law of gravity? I was perplexed, stumped, and (for one of the few times in my life) at a loss for words.

We all know that as time marches on, gravity is what takes us down and makes us older. 25 years later, I realize now the answer was elusive and evasive. But there was a substitute explanation, and I decided that he was right.

I can't defy the laws of gravity, but I can use it to my advantage. In thousands of ways, this is how man doubled up his ability to create more energy: by using gravity with a fulcrum tool, hydraulics, waterfalls, and other ways that engineers have utilized.

As a human, you can capitalize on gravity by lifting weights, looking better and therefore giving you the advantage over people who don't. Without gravity, you can't gain muscle mass or look better than someone who doesn't. This is why astronauts in outer space come back weak and flabby. This means gravity is as much your friend if you turn a negative into a positive as it is your enemy.

Gravity isn't the only force that we can use energy on to subdue and overpower. You'll want to approach the question of whether gravity is even related to energy.

Even your mind and the decisions that are processed in the brain require energy. Instead of 'brain', let's use the word 'device', much like you have a computer that runs on electrical energy. When you get an answer from Google on your computer, you have just powered a solar battery to 110V.

The human mind runs on millions and millions of neurotransmitters that are bathed in an electrical solution. This produces an easy flow or conduit, allowing messages, information and ideas to travel to and fro. This flow of electrical current allows you to fire a question, then receive answers inside your brain without using Google.

Stop and think about your car's battery, and how it produces power to run your engine and how it's full of liquid. Like Google, the answers are available inside your mind, much like they're programmed into your Google service. The difference in the human mind and Google is that Google had to be programmed with answers. These answers are done by a superior source: the human mind.

This supernatural possession we call a 'mind' can find its own conclusions or answers. Man is the only creature that can build a flying machine then calculate the required distances to travel into space.

To take this one step further and show the difference, man is also the only creature that can find a problem to solve. Science is at the precipice of producing artificial intelligence with the claimed capability of replicating human reasoning and logic. This leads to the possibility of making humans antiquated and of no value. This, of course, will negate any reason for you to have reasoning and to think for yourself. This is where we are headed.

Will science someday change this paradigm that exists today, where computers are subservient to us? Yes, the possibility of making us slaves to them exists. This once again proves man's folly when trying to be God.

Inside this device we call a brain, we get our sexual preferences, all of our likes and dislikes, our loves and our fears and many other characteristics. Man appears to be the only species that is aware of his consciousness and that someday, he will die.

Science is still resistant to the supernatural in the human brain, a superior being that separate us from all other life on the planet. This resistance is inherent in all of mankind because it necessitates guidance that removes your control, and it removes man receiving all the credit. If there had been no supernatural reasoning programmed into the human mind, we would be similar to a laptop without Windows, a hard drive, a processor, or Google.

This is where I will anger a lot of scientists, atheists, and medical doctors. They have decided that if you can't see, weigh, touch or measure an item, it doesn't exist. This is not to say that many physicians don't believe in a supernatural force for healing.

Scholars and scientists as well as microbiologists concur that the brain runs on electricity. Of course, so does your television, your automobile, and your computer. Keep in mind that you cannot see the electricity that runs these devices. But ask any electrician, they'll tell you not to touch a live wire. If you challenge them because you can't see electricity, you will soon get the literal shock of your life.

Even before there was electricity or before it was understood and utilized by science, the Holy Bible clarified this with a scripture. The scripture I am referring to says that faith is the substance of things unseen. Now, did you get that thousands of years ago, the prophets knew faith was an invisible force that would motivate good versus evil? Faith permeates every part of your life yet is invisible to the human eye, not because it is too small to see, but because its presence can only be seen in its results. This is the same way the wind causes the trees to move: you only see the result of the wind, but not the wind.

We are going to examine some of the negative things that occur in the human mind when exposed to drugs. Just like you can short-circuit your laptop with water, get the wrong answer, or make the wrong decision, drugs can do this to the human mind. There is no doubt that the human mind is the most powerful and valuable possession that ever existed. Without the mind, there would absolutely be no advancements, no space race, no hospitals to heal the sick, no churches to adjust your character or attitude. Without the mind, there would be no difference between man and any other animal on Earth. Without the mind we would not see or recognize a universe

If you believe this about the mind, and if it is the most precious possession that we have, then why are we abusing it? I have no intentions in this book of playing God or judging anyone, but I do have the intention of pointing out the importance of your mind. It is so important to you, it may be the vehicle or the force that takes you into eternity. You don't have to be Christian, Islamic, Buddhist, or any other religion to have this knowledge.

Universal sanity is predicated and contingent upon you making good decisions with this mind. In all religions, theologies or beliefs, there are requirements that you must commit to while living on this planet to achieve promised immortality. These requirements are similar, but also have differences in their doctrines and theology. They share one common thread: character. For the most part, it has to be pretty good to acquire immortality.

This is the reason why the human mind has the ability to take you into eternity, just as much as your car has the ability to take you to California. It is up to you to find the right belief system that works with your mind and not against it.

I find it strange and perplexing that Islam demands the murder of all other religious people who don't believe their doctrines. It shouldn't take a rocket scientist to know that is not a sane religion, but an attempt to be God by judgment. This is why many theologians consider Islam a type of antiChrist movement prophesied.

Why do we say that the human brain is the most powerful force on this planet? Neurotransmitters in the brain fire back and forth between cells at the speed of thought. The size and distances between these neurotransmitters are relevant compared to the distances of space and stars. This relevance of speed is faster than the speed of light because it travels at the speed of thought.

The same brain, the same mind that you possess, is the same type of device that split the atom and produced atomic power and weapons. Similarly, the human mind produced kidney dialysis, the polio vaccine, and the mapping of the human genome along with medical cures.

One could make the argument that the human brain or mind is a microcosm of the universe. After all, it contains the correct distances from cell to cell as the distance between stars to planets and galaxies.

Paranormalists as well as some astronomers believe this is the reason we have cosmic connections with the universe. This begs this question: Is the universe aware of its existence, and is it held together by a similar force?

Of course, we are only having fun with physics. It is a break from this serious subjects of drugs, the brain, and the mind.

The thought processes in the brain are the reason why we have telescopes, we went to the moon, and we're exploring outer space. If you remove the order created in the human brain, you have a world that doesn't make sense or can become chaotic. Nothing can happen and be appreciated or condemned if it's bad or good without reasoning in the human mind. The same elements and chemicals furnished inside your brain are prevalent throughout the universe, and are in the same quantities—a fact overlooked by scientists.

Mozart, Beethoven, Bach, or even Elvis could never have been appreciated for their artistry without the unseen forces behind the human mind. Of course, without their minds, these same artists would never have had the imagination and creativity to produce the works that we love and enjoy.

Animals can also learn, but only by repetitive rewards furnished in nature or by training with rewards only.

If man is contained by three-dimensional physics from ascertaining certain knowledge at this time, is there a reason? There appears to be limits on mankind regarding doors we should or not open concerning knowledge. The first example of this was posted and listed in Genesis, when Eve was forbidden to eat a certain fruit of the tree of good and evil and/or knowledge. Scholars or theologians will concur that this account in Genesis was a metaphor that spoke about things that are just not to be known by man while in this dimension. Astrophysicist, paranormalists as well as religious leaders believe we are being guided by supernatural entities.

The human mind has now revealed that travel through wormholes by bending time and space may be possible. This same device called a brain has produced the capability to destroy and annihilate all life through nuclear weapons. What causes some to turn to death and destruction by their decisions, and some to turn to decisions that will feed millions and heal the sick?

It is also with our minds that we make love beyond our biology, which only responds to the mind. Otherwise, we could get turned on while thinking of a tree or a cloud.

Drugs can open a Pandora's box of sexual deviation and evil that can create a lifetime of pain, if allowed. Drugs like meth, crack or roofies can create sexual results that can last a lifetime; and with deadly negative consequences. Many STDs are fueled by drugs which erase caution and common sense. The wrong kind of drug can cause a normal person to perpetrate a sexual crime that will shame them for life.

Some of these sex crimes also ruin the lives of the victims they assault. These sexual crimes can range from sodomy, rape, sexual murder or pedophilia—all of which can be unleashed in a mind under the influence of meth or other drugs.

There are, of course, many crimes that are sexual in nature; and where quite often, the result is death. While deciding between sex and the brain's influence as to whether or not you had normal or perverted sex, just use common sense.

A clean mind free of drugs will usually make the right decisions based on moderation. One way you can always measure yourself concerning sex is if you feel guilty after sex. If you do, you probably are

Sexual preferences have been recorded since Biblical time. They are a personal matter between you and your Creator. I have no problem with going on record and stating adamantly that I am against same-sex marriage, and that is my personal opinion. As to why you're either heterosexual, bisexual, or homosexual, the decision to be one or the other can be influenced by many variables.

One thing's for certain: drugs only complicate your life, no matter your sexuality. If drugs are involved, they will facilitate and create a lifetime of consequences and scars. Your development years (when you are growing emotionally, physically, and spiritually) are when you are the most vulnerable and likely to develop lifetime preferences.

If sex occurs and you are still a child, this unnatural and untimely event can destroy the natural flow of time and development and rob you of a normal life. If it is true, we cannot attach drug use directly to this problem; but it is obviously a contributing factor that's rarely admitted or reported. During this time, not protecting your child from sexual predators and drugs simultaneously can produce a double-edged sword of pain, suffering and emotional stress that will haunt that child forever.

I think this problem speaks about how naïve the American family has been for the last 60 years, or since the end of World War II.

In William Shakespeare's play *Hamlet*, Polonius said: "To thine own self be true." No better example comes to mind than sexual truth and clarity. The fact is that drugs will open a Pandora's box of sexual perversions that a sound mind would not embrace. Some things aren't negotiable, in the same way sexual pedophilia is not negotiable. It is wrong according to the letter of the law, and according to spiritual and moral decency.

Will there come a time in America when sexual pedophilia will be accepted and defended by marches, like same-sex marriage? Will this mean that because of political correctness, the day will come when America cannot call a child molester what he or she is?

 Drugs can interrupt a normal path of passion, remove your inhibitions, and open up logic that will morph into dangerous behavior. I am not trying to be square; and if you are a hetero couple who wants to swing from the chandeliers, as long as it's confined to consenting adults, who's to judge?

To encapsulate this narrative and to simplify things, I am not trying to police or push my way of life. This is between you and your Creator, if you believe you have one.

If you are a gay couple and you want to swing from the chandeliers once again, that is your right. I only ask that you not try to force your thinking or marriage beliefs on me. If you are a gay person and can show scriptures that condone gay marriage, you should put it in every newspaper. If you're a heterosexual or a gay couple, and drugs are in use, before long, you will throw your inhibitions, guidelines, and caution to the wind.

Many scholars, psychiatrists, and medical doctors will tell you that some of our sexual deviations are learned characteristics. One thing is for certain: all sexual behavior and preferences can turn to evil when drugs are involved.

You should now be seeing a picture of a mind that produces every thought and decision. This book isn't about sex, but about how drugs interfere with the mind.

Now, we have explained and adequately shown that sex and the mind are connected somewhat more than just through our genitalia. Some of my readers will misconstrue and think that I am judging and condemning them for a sexual lifestyle. Nothing could be further from the truth. I am only showing the influence of drugs in every category of life; and if you will tell the truth to yourself, you will know I am right.

If you take offense, that is your right. I am not good enough to judge, nor would you be.

Know this: the book I have been endorsing, the Holy Bible, is adamant that anyone can be forgiven when they correct bad sexual habits. At that point, I have to refer to what Jesus told the woman at the well. She was forgiven; "Go and sin no more." This necessitates that you stop whatever you're doing wrong, especially if it's wrong and hurting someone who's innocent. Believe it or not, that someone can be you.

No matter how far left or right your political views or your status in life are, there are absolutes that we must obey. This includes sexual barriers. Even the animal kingdom recognizes the laws of nature because there are consequences when we break them. A sex life facilitated by drugs that leads to rape or sodomy may land you in prison. Gang members such as MS-13 have perpetrated horrible, heinous sex acts on innocent women, men and children while using drugs. To say that "the mind is a terrible thing to waste" is an understatement. It's also a terrible thing to pervert or destroy.

We've all have lucid dreams while under the influence of rapid eye movement or REM sleep. These dreams are a mysterious part of the brain that can be very revealing. Just as we did not understand radar before World War II or its benefits, we do not understand dreams and their ability to reveal and see the future. Of course, from a military and scientific standpoint, radar can see the enemy coming before you see them with your eyes. The only difference in these two sources is that one is understood electronically and meteorologically, while the other is still considered supernatural and unpolished science.

This process of REM sleep can take us to places in the mind that we can't access in our normal reality. One thing that paranormalists, spiritualists as well as science must admit is that you can't help what you dream. Most psychiatrists, medical doctors, and parapsychologists will concur that we only utilize 10% of our brain's capacity. If that is true, this means we have 90% more that remains untapped and available.

One might wonder what is preventing us from using all of our learning capacity. I surmise this other 90% of capability waiting in the human mind will be accessible after we become spiritual as opposed to biological. The answer is not so simple, but most logic points to the fact that it is because we live in a three-dimensional world. If this logic is true, this means our mind and its capabilities have been partially contained because of three-dimensional physics. This, of course, could mean that the other 90% is attached to a more supernatural part of the human existence. This also explains why as we sleep, our metabolic systems shut down, almost to the point of death.

Much like radar, we can access this other dimension that can actually warn us about things or scenarios in the future. Even when King Nebuchadnezzar insisted that Daniel interpret his dream, he was demanding that he look into the future. As humans, we are subject to the laws of three-dimensional physics. In our molecular structure, there are barriers that we cannot transcend. But the human brain and the mind are not confined, limited or contained in a three-dimensional physical existence like our bodies.

As we mentioned earlier, certain drugs usually open the mind in a negative way. Some artists, songwriters, poets, and even scientific achievements or breakthroughs are often produced by a mind on drugs; and not all of it is good. Hitler and his control over the masses with almost-supernatural oracle skills was fueled by methamphetamine. There are thousands of accounts in recent and ancient history of the masses being persuaded to go the wrong way because of drugs.

This most powerful instrument that we have described as the mind is really more powerful than nuclear energy. There is nothing else on Earth that's powerful enough to compare to the mind itself. You can forget taking your biological bodies to other planetary systems without this powerful device we call the brain or the mind.

Much of the medical field will split company with me whenever I use the term 'brain' or 'mind'. This is because one is biological and the other is supernatural. This is exactly what I am implying; not to know this would be equivalent to believing that other characteristics of a mind are biological, and we know they're not. If that were true, you would see hate, love, faith, distrust, any and all emotional states and the results of behavior from those emotional states.

Of course, there will be those who believe the human mind has no supernatural capabilities, and that it is just a product of evolution. I surmise and I believe that 90% of my readers feel the distinction, or can differentiate between their biology and feelings produced in that same mind.

Eastern religions, Christianity, and most all other spiritualists embrace this idea of the unseen. My objective is not to replace Darwin's theory or so-called science; it is to point out the potholes that can destroy your brain, spirit and mind with drugs. There is an attack and attempt like no other time in history to destroy this supernatural entity in your mind that produces good results. This attack on our minds is being implemented by forces of evil that have existed for eons. The tool they use the most is drugs; what better tampering mechanism than drugs to disrupt an destroy sanity?

Ask anyone who has come off of drugs after months in jail or rehab and are back home or on the streets. These recovering addicts will tell you it's almost supernatural how individuals find and approach them with drugs, no matter how well they hide. These individuals are now experts, and they're right; it's not just coincidence that these drug dealers are always in the right place and time.

America, I'll tell you on good authority that the last 40 years has produced these insane and bizarre crimes (and in greater numbers) because of drug dealers. I know there will be those who will argue that murders and bizarre crimes have always occurred, but this process is now a bloody chain that connects us from coast to coast.

For decades, there were subliminal messages that have been embraced. One of these is that we should all live for the moment. This idea about sexual freedoms ("to each his own") that started in the '60s came with the drug epidemic. So did diseases. Millions are a part of this deception and this promotion of evil, and are not even aware of it because it has crept in and accepted without their knowledge.

This slow and subtle approach is used in every form of drug sales and by street dealers. The motive, to create murder and mayhem instead of peace and love, lies in malevolent entities that are not of this world. Their plan is to disrupt, destroy and subvert a plan set forth by God and His family many thousands of years ago. Drugs are used to facilitate this process. I am not saying that all crimes are Satanic or are caused by evil beings, so let's not give them too much credit.

There is a beginning to every journey, so small crimes always grow with drug use until it is morphed into headlines; and they are never good. What begin as small crimes will eventually become larger until the human mind is a willing participant. This powerful force, the mind, is not to be abused; it is to be guarded. No amount of armaments would be as good as sound intelligence and logic.

As a reader, the source or the foundation of all knowledge concerning your mind, spirit, and soul is in the Holy Bible. It is an owner's manual for the human mind. The God Family is working with a timetable concerning mankind here on Earth. Wisdom and knowledge that you garner out of the holy scriptures in your Bible are the new GPS that has been available for all of recorded history. Don't let drugs short it out.

Chapter 6

Deception

Yes, the most advanced and privileged nation that has ever existed is also the most deceived. You are a part of an unparalleled prosperity that allows every citizen to live like kings would have 100 years ago. We are a nation with a military which is more powerful than that of China, Russia, or all other nations combined. No one in their right mind would attack us militarily.

If this is all true, why are we in danger and dying from a domestic, man-made, self-inflicted epidemic?

As you can see, the title of this chapter points to deception from within and outside our nation. It's time to tell the truth, starting with the one word that describes every political party: deception.

Deception now permeates almost all major news networks. These news networks no longer report the news, but are the news because of their fake and ulterior motives. If they could be stopped from spreading lies and falsifying news reports, it would be dangerous. This is a very tricky maneuver, one that can backfire; and their response would be that it's a violation of their First Amendment rights.

It appears that the free press and major news networks are systematically using the bill of rights to destroy the Bill of Rights. Of course, it is true that we have the right to say whatever we want; it's called 'freedom of speech', and for that, we're fortunate.

The consequences can be great if it's deception. Americans are not fooled or stupid; most see through this fake-media narrative that permeates many major channels. These fake and subversive news accounts are an effort to subvert and undermine America. In my opinion, these false narratives are many times worse than anything any president has ever done. This is tantamount to treason on a level never before seen. Remember, news channels have your ear like no one else.

The reason I say it's worse is because the president is only one person. There are literally thousands of journalists, anchors, and correspondents who use their news outlets for political subversion. No, I'm not talking about the possible sale of uranium that Hillary Clinton signed off on and helped to facilitate.

Why these accusations have not been addressed or adamantly been pursued goes to the exact heart of this chapter. Here, we are looking for bad players right under our nose whom we trusted and voted for.

It appears that during the last couple of years of the Obama Administration, a leading DEA agent was told to stand down on money laundering and enormous drug deals. At the very least, the agent was dissuaded from pursuing the largest investigated hit concerning drugs and money laundering in American history. Keep in mind that the DEA's job is to investigate money laundering and prosecute kingpins, small and large, in America and abroad.

Derek Maltz, the chief investigator for a $200-million-a-month money laundering investigation, was stifled, contained, and prevented from procuring the final results. This investigation concerned Hezbollah, a terrorist organization connected to ISIS .

 It appears this was one of the largest money laundering investigations in American history. But it wasn't pursued adamantly by Holder for fear of offending and collapsing the Iranian nuclear deal.

This plan that was masked by an automobile assistance program for Africa turned into a money laundering scheme to finance

Hezbollah. This financed their terrorist activities around the world, according to this major DEA agent; and provided weapons with some money deals masked by this car assistance program. According to the agent, the money was used by ISIS and Hezbollah to buy heroin to sell in America.

As to whether or not President Obama was aware of this, only history will tell. Obama didn't want to jeopardize his already-bad deal with Iran, so the issue was never raised. But the Iranian deal was subsequently dismantled.

According to Agent Maltz, Hezbollah, ISIS, Hamas, and other terrorist groups delivering heroin to America were financed with this deal. Why would America allow Hezbollah to make hundreds of millions from the sale of heroin that kills your children? These Islamic terrorists put these drugs on the streets with money from the Iranian regime that loves our prosperity; but hates everything else about America, including its people. Hopefully, by the time this book is published, President Donald Trump would not have been impeached by the deep-state forces that are trying to block his efforts.

Although this is startling revelation concerning the Obama presidency, it's not the only one. It appears that all presidencies in the last 30 years allowed this epidemic to explode, with no serious efforts to stop it. The presidents who preceded Obama (at least the last four) should have their legacies challenged. Our former leaders who were supposed to protect the American people are all guilty of allowing Islamists to sell heroin to your children.

The Obama Administration deliberately relaxed immigration requirements concerning terrorist-connected nations all across the world. If you came from an Islamic nation where 99% of all terrorists are from, you were more than welcome during Obama's tenure. This administration made it easier for Islamists to acquire citizenship in America than any other president in history.

Also during Obama's administration, Islamic immigration increased by 400%. This is the reason why mosques are being built all across America, and they are very militaristic about their privacy. Compare this to American churches that have very open-door policies and invite the public with open arms.

There are many prominent intellectuals in America who believe this is an enormous Trojan horse waiting to strike America from within. We have been shown how their religious doctrine demands your death unless you agree to this ideology. You can't make these things up; look up statistics and read history books.

Islamists extremists have infiltrated our schools, medical facilities, political and monetary systems; they now have a persuasive grip on America. While they hide in the shadows and are protected by our religious freedom, are they are planning to overthrow America?

If you think this is too far-right, don't forget that the Islamic murders at Fort Hood, Texas were perpetrated by someone with the same beliefs, or thousands more like it. This killer was going through military training and waiting to strike at the core of our military. He could not contain his hatred for Christianity, our sovereignty, and America's way of life any longer.

This was a microcosm of what lies in wait throughout our nation, and indeed was a Trojan horse attack. We have seen this scenario played out thousands of times across the world; and when they are in our country, no matter where they exist, they don't change stripes.

These Islamists are protected by our institutions and freedoms, but are disguised as a Trojan horse with their belief system and motives intact. Look back over the last 40 years; you will see that 99% of foreign and domestic terrorism is done by extremists born out of Islam.

When we think of bad or failed leadership, we are thinking of our government, our president, Congress, and (for the most part) all politicians. It would be nice if it was only our government; but Americans are deceived, misled, killed and murdered by almost every high-ranking profession that exists. Most Americans follow a higher moral platform that hates dishonesty but have witnessed this accepted behavior from our leaders for the past 5 to 6 decades.

American logic says if it's okay for the clergy, doctors or politicians to lie and garner wealth. Why not the plumber, electrician or mechanic? It gets worse; the medical field has done the most damage, maybe more than any other profession.

We are going to expose in this chapter people who have told us any and everything that our ears were itching to hear. After they told us lies, they took everything, from our mental to our physical well-being. In some cases, our lives, our health, and the health of those we love more than ourselves have been taken, too. Page by page, we will expose the perpetrators their motives, and even look into their minds.

You can take a man's money or his property; but when you murder his family, you cross the line and will get a response. This murder of the American people has been occurring now for 60 years, in enormous numbers. It is time for you, the American people, to know the truth and to react.

Deception is a Biblical term, as you know. It goes back to spiritual beings as far back in recorded history or as the Book of Genesis can take us.

In Matthew, Christ's disciples approached him and said, "Tell us, what will be a sign of the end of the world?" (Or, better translated in the Greek and Hebrew: end of an age.)

Jesus did not hesitate. He said, "Deception. Take heed that no man deceive you, for many will come in my name, claiming I am the Christ. But yet, they will deceive many."

Notice that he did not say they would deny that he was Christ. In fact, he admitted they would acknowledge this point, and they do today.

After deception, the other chronological events that Christ itemized were seismic events like earthquakes, volcanoes, wars, diseases, and pestilence. However, there was something different about war that would separate the modern world from antiquity: it seems Christ mentioned a new kind of war. Christ stated that unless he returned at a certain time, there would be no flesh left alive on Earth. But for the elect's sake, he would return in time.

Keep in mind that when he made that prophecy, there wasn't even a light bulb on this planet. At no other time in history did man ever have the capability to destroy all human flesh. We do today. Therefore, we must conclude this was advance notice of nuclear weapons 2,000 years ago.

If you tune in to any T.V. evangelist's program, the number-one narrative and theme that will dominate their broadcast will be the law of giving; of course, they are the recipients. Our clergy or evangelicals have not spoken out and exposed the truth, nor even addressed the problem that is killing more of our youth than anything else. This is because this doesn't put any money in their pocket, and it takes time away from their visits to the bank. Just like our politicians, the clergy have become either good at deception or bad theologians. No one knows the number of young people who have died better than the clergy; after all who preaches their funerals? This is a very sad subject matter that doesn't put a lot of money into the church's foundation box.

I find it strange and ironic that most evangelists and preachers talk about prosperity just as much as the fake news networks talk about Russian collusion.

There was a time in America when if you had a family problem, you could go to the church and get understanding, a blessing, and help. Deception, money, and greed in our religious foundations have created a new type of church that has morphed into cults in some cases that not only not help your child, but take advantage of them.

This narrative that almost all megachurches push 24/ 7 has created more hopeless in drug users and alienated many. America, the drug epidemic has put millions of children on the streets, lost and estranged from their parents. The church may no longer be a sanctuary, but part of the problem.

No, I am not saying that all churches fit this description. But there has been an enormous number of preachers and pastors who have capitalized on your child's addiction. These churches look for kids who fit a criteria of emotional trauma and stress produced by a family that has been destroyed by the drug epidemic. These cults that have emerged in the last 40 years can take control, use and abuse them just as badly as a drug dealer.

Many operate like the psychiatrist who treats your troubled child, then turns them into a cash register. Some religious groups capitalize on your child's emotional stress to extract cash and to create a new type of family. There is a quite similar paradigm that appears between psychiatrists, psychologists and the clergy when capitalizing on an emotional child. One of their objectives is to prevent unification between your child and you or any family members.

When a church organization recruits a young person who is already naïve and wounded by emotional trauma, they are like putty in their hands. They will use them by the thousands or as many as they can recruit, and make the church leaders the new family.

You will also find that if a young person is badly addicted to drugs, some churches don't want them because they only want the cream of the crop. A characteristic you can always look for in a cult is the effort to make you feel they have privileged knowledge, and no one but them have it.

This appeals to a young person's vanity and makes sense, but it get worse. This will be followed up by informing you that you are special, or that no one else can understand you like they can. The next thing they will do is to inform you that all your problems and your drug use are results of your childhood and abuse.

Many children are abused at a young age. But in many cases, they are also made to believe something happened when it never occurred. This immediately estranges parents from their children, who really are usually the only real people you can trust in life. This process of deception lets the dealers who created the problem off the hook, and allows the clergy to estrange their new recruits from their family.

Nothing is more fun or more rewarding than a new religious recruit getting to play the victim. They will feed on it until it becomes a part of their DNA. It isn't that they're not a victim, but they become a part of a bigger problem by blaming the wrong people. They now become victims of the church, the street dealers, the pharmaceutical industry, or all three.

Once these charismatic church leaders hijack your child's mind, you are very unlikely to get them back. At this point, the child's psychological situation becomes similar to what's known as Stockholm Syndrome. America used this term in the Patty Hearst kidnapping case in the '60s. Quite often, these young women will fall in love with church pastors, preachers, or any other authority figures in this organization.

This phenomenon has grown in America alongside the drug epidemic. If your child is taken out of your control, a state-sponsored psychiatrist may recommend medication. This profession will only further alienate you from your child; this almost guarantees you will never get them back. This also generates paychecks for state-appointed doctors or anyone employed by the state, and sells expensive pharmaceutical mind-control drugs.

This means that if your child was emotionally traumatized and addicted by drug dealers, the next set of drug dealers will now have their turn and have a license. This next drug dealer, the medical field, dispenses powerful narcotics and pharmaceuticals like Prozac, Zoloft, and an entire list of psychotic drugs, all very expensive.

In reality, the clergy and the medical field both hold control and money over your child. Quite often, someone has to be the bad guy to justify this control. You, as the parent, are quite often an innocent target. Many of these young people are bounced around like in a pinball machine by doctors or used by clergy and state-sponsored hospitals until they are used up. While church leaders or so-called medical experts are collecting tens of millions from thousands of recruits from the government, you as a parent are often villainized.

I am telling you this with sadness and disappointment, but we've already said the truth will be told. This is a big problem, and it means our sacred institutions of Christianity and our medical industry have capitalized on wounded kids and the drug epidemic. But I still believe in America's religious institutions, and would choose to trust them over any other institution.

We have already shown and quoted Christ in the Book of Matthew about this deception by those who profess their existence the most. The agenda of fake news and the liberal agenda is to take America apart brick by brick, principle by principle. The goal to destroy our past, and then implement a system that will mesh us into a world with no individualism.

The spiritual beings described in ancient texts have a motive: to destroy and take away your human potential. Their tool is deception facilitated by drugs, and is designed to take away your three-dimensional existence on Earth, and possibly your eternity. There are powerful entities that do not care about money. These forces do not need money, but they realize you do. Therefore, they play on your character with deception that can destroy or control your life. They use money and greed to compromise your character by deception. It starts from the top and works its way down. This spiritual hierarchy affects us from the highest to the lowest, and the consequences are like gravity. But the results are death and destruction.

Evil forces have always used money as a tool to tempt the players that existed at that time. Now, it's drugs. Look at Judas Iscariot and what he did for 30 pieces of silver; or Delilah, who betrayed Samson to the Philistines for 1,100 silver coins. Money is always the first temptation.

Let's not worry about what happened thousands of years ago; your time on this planet is right now. The threats that you are encountering are current and deadly.

America, please do not misunderstand. This nation was built, founded, and predicated on freedom of religion and belief in God. Nothing could ever dissuade or stop me from protecting Judeo-Christian freedoms and institutions, but even they need a reprimand about this epidemic.

Tens of thousands of churches dot the landscape from coast to coast in America, with millions of members who could be of use to assist in this epidemic. Most of America's religious institutions are filled with good, decent people; and are a safe place to donate. But when the powerful and wealthy evangelists began using radio and T.V., a supernatural door opened. These were supposed to send the gospel to every ear and nation on the planet. It is sad, but it is also true: many (not all, but many) have perverted and used that worldwide electronic door to provide personal wealth.

Religious professionals or pastors are not the only people we are taught to trust. For so long in America, we have been taught we can trust the medical field and that it has our best interest at heart. We now know that the medical field, including the pharmaceutical industry, is motivated by money and greed. Evidence suggests that 30% of operations and diagnoses are done not to cure you, but to make the attorney, doctor and the pharmaceutical industry wealthy. In many cases, these operations can cost you your life or limbs, but these will always fill the pockets of those in the medical industry

When it is recommended that you have surgery for any number of reasons, it is guaranteed to be a $5,000 to $100,000 profit for these pros. Hospitals, X-ray technicians, laboratory techs and rehabilitation centers will also get rich from these overly zealous diagnoses.

There was a time in history when newspapers, radio and T.V. were your greatest assets in protecting your freedoms. Even gangsters, bank robbers, or anyone else would go to the newspaper headquarters to turn themselves in and wait for the sheriff. The one thing America relies on is this one-eyed monster that sits in every home, called a television. Most Americans trust what we see and hear on T.V. because we can't fathom that the media would lie. It's not that the American people don't realize that they lie; we just can't see their motive.

America, I am afraid that I must inform you the free press is no longer free. The so-called free press that you hear and see every day could cost you more than money. In their minds, they have justified lying to you, the American people, in order to achieve the goals of those who are behind there agenda. Their original intent and purpose was to report the news, and not to be the news. This process is financed by the global elitists to achieve their agenda, wherein billions will eventually be controlled by only a few.

Their agenda and motive are even more sinister and dangerous than the love of money. Some of the powerful Main Street media are in bed with globalists in China. You might be asking yourself at this point: What does this have to do with being on drugs? The answer is sad and dangerous. When 45% of Americans are physically and emotionally incapacitated because of drugs, they are easily controlled.

Ask yourself this, America: Where do the billionaires, the elite, the globalists get their money? These globalists get their money from you, the masses, who are struggling and carve out an existence on $20,000 to $60,000 a year. When we buy an automobile, a washer and dryer or anything, it is you, the masses, who make billionaires out of these worldwide businessmen.

This doesn't necessarily mean that all billionaires are globalists or that you are a part of this agenda. It is the intent of this book not to just wake up the blue-collar worker, but those who own American industry. There isn't anything wrong with being a globalist as long as it isn't a replacement for patriotism, sovereignty and freedom.

A new and emerging socialist party would love to see all billionaires stripped of their wealth and then distributed to the average person. This kind of thinking will destroy the greatest nation and the greatest freedom that ever existed. It has been tried throughout modern history, with no success for centuries.

As you sit at home in your comfortable chair and you watch football, wrestling or soap operas, you are being controlled. Millions are being controlled and indoctrinated to think in a certain way by the major news networks and commercials. They have created an opportunity where your mind is in neutral to influence you, and they never miss an opportunity. When you are disengaged mentally, you are vulnerable; and the tool they use is distraction.

This doesn't account for nor does it include the technology that exists today and is being used to watch you when you are watching T.V. Yes, believe it or not, it is possible that you are being watched by your television as much as you are watching it.

There isn't anything evil about advertising, but it has lent itself with its tricks of the trade to the elite globalist. These revolutionaries want to control your thought patterns and buying habits through the new science of algorithms. You will notice that there's always a pharmaceutical commercial aired during every big sporting event or primetime T.V. program. These advertisements promise different drugs that will make life better and you, more youthful. Acceptance is their goal. If you can accept news about murders, rapes and heinous crimes without resisting, then you are in the throes of complacency.

Most of us enjoy slight monetary gains from time to time, and are programmed to believe that life is okay and things aren't that bad. We are taught to follow each other like sheep to the slaughter, and to never question our footsteps. This slow, methodical trajectory will allow the globalist to control the entire planet and make you subservient, with no individuality and no sovereignty, within just a few more years. This is the reason why the globalists have been in favor of increased populations or more people to buy their products.

It is time to open your eyes, remove the veil, take off your matrix helmet, and come back to reality with powerful individual thinking. Look around your world. Ask about the preservatives and poisons that are in our food to our pharmaceutical industry. Then you will see this process of deception. America, you are asleep or partially comatose, intoxicated and chained into a struggle just to survive.

Political correctness is used by liberals to make you believe they are protecting you and making the world more fair and balanced. The reality is that they keep you in this matrix and sedated with a feeling that is designed to prevent you from resisting. That is the narrative of fake news and elites and are used to make you compliant. If you resist, you are racist or against women and gays, leaving you with no freedom to choose. These freedoms cover everything from abortion to gay rights and (I believe, soon) pedophilia. The truth is they figured out a way to conquer and divide America that will steal your individuality. The world Globalist while making you as a minority feel like a victim are really playing you as a pawn in a chess game for your future . I believe America's minority population will surprise these world players and take control of their God given rights .

Our food that we pay dearly for makes us sick, then our medical industry treats us with drugs that we also pay dearly for. This process never gets to the problem; but it treats the effects, only causing addiction. Stopping or curing the cause of manmade illnesses would not generate repeat business or sell pharmaceuticals.

If you take sugar alone and realize that it is responsible for 60% of all bad health, you will begin to open your eyes and realize the problem. Our food industries put this ingredient in everything from ketchup, oranges, and potato chips. 95% of all processed food is full of sugar. We are now a nation of sugar addicts, and sugar has the capability to kill more Americans in the long haul than cancer. After a diabetic diagnosis, we realize that we are just as addicted to sugar in all its forms as the junkie on the street is to his heroin. No one can claim this process was planned, or if it evolved and was then taken advantage of by the wealthy. Either way, the consequences are the same.

America's security infrastructure, police force, hospitals and surveillance systems as well as funeral industry are prosperous and predicated on drugs and drug violence. Attorneys, bail bondsmen, prisons and jails thrive from this process of addiction that now exists.

If all of America's sales of pharmaceuticals and street drugs ceases to exist, we would actually have economic collapse. Drugs have fueled our economy in a negative way that our legislators and our economists won't admit.

Pharmaceutical drugs have fueled the economy in another negative way: by creating deaths and lawsuits. Only recently have our legislators given this epidemic the validity and seriousness that are overdue. Our president, Donald Trump, is the first person I've seen in my lifetime to actually take this seriously.

Billionaires who are not on drugs make more millions because of inner-city crime and drugs. When neighborhoods are riddled with crime, commercial and residential real estate zoning and property values decline. This makes these properties an easy snatch, buy and flip for the globalists from China to the Middle East. It's obvious; when you live in cities like Dallas, Chicago or any modern metropolitan area and you do drugs, this is what happens.

Law enforcement, attorneys, bail bondsmen and the medical field make money from gunshots or overdoses. Security firms sell anything and everything related to inner-city crime for years until drugs win, then property values collapse over time.

After years of drug use that definitely spreads to your family and friends, your health will fail. Next, you will go to jail and lose everything financially, emotionally, physically, and even spiritually when this occurs. After addiction and prison time, the entire infrastructure is based and predicated on you screwing up your probation, making it a revolving door.

After all of the above has happened in life and you have aged 30 years in 10, the globalists and the billionaires buy up the properties. As we just mentioned, real estate would be a cheap flip for the globalists from China or even America because of crime. These communities would be where you and your family once lived and attended school. It would also be where many friends died from this epidemic. If you get to stay in the neighborhood, you are relegated to a life of subservience. At this point, you will have no choice but to pay for your probation and medical bills after you get out of the hospital or prison.

After reading this chapter, you will either be on the side that has not yet done drugs, or (if you have done drugs) you will stop. Hopefully, this will make sense. But if you are like the millions who have done drugs and your life is already ruined, it will make even more sense. If you are the one of the few who only experimented and you haven't ruined your life with drugs, you are lucky.

Knowledge and an understanding of right and wrong always wins out in the universe. This explanation is as close as it can get to a magic bullet or crystal ball that most only listen to after suffering losses.

For those of you who have done drugs and lost it all but still have your life, your commission is to point out the potholes to those who stand where you once stood. This may be the only form of redemption you ever achieve, but it's a good feeling and it will makes you whole again. All of this evil can be stopped if you read exposés and explain to your loved ones what you know about drugs that either cross our borders or those we have domestically.

Chapter 7

If Money Fails

When man began to use agriculture instead of hunting and gathering, groups formed around water and settled near rivers or natural lakes. Modern man still coalesces around water, even in an age when we can travel to the far ends of the solar system.

As man began to barter, it didn't take long to realize that a cow or a bushel of potatoes were heavy; and so is water carried for long distances. This is why there was a need to have something that you could carry in your pockets that would buy your needs. At first, these were trinkets, jewelry or gold—anything that was small but had value. The one thing that makes anything like gold valuable is scarcity: it's hard to make or find. As civilizations developed, man made coins that were crude; but these would replace bartering.

Man is always looking for a more efficient, clever, and foolproof technique of buying and selling. This is proof that globalization has its roots in antiquity. Before electricity was harnessed or even discovered, modern coins were in use. Governments probably came up with the idea to use cash or coins to make taxing the people easier. I am sure that 7,000 years ago, there were people like me who did not trust their government and consulted each other in private about this shifty new way of buying and selling with currency.

Of course, we have now stepped into cryptocurrency and all of the different and still-evolving strategies and angles that would benefit the government. We now live in a nanotech society that has the capability to track every human being on Earth. The current infrastructure is capable of tracking your every move; and knowing your whereabouts, spending habits, sexual preferences, or any personal information, even how you think.

Their objective to take us from primitive cash to something even more convenient... but for who?

There are more sinister and evil parts of this story that we will get into. And yes, believe it or not, it is one of the tentacles of the drug epidemic, and one of the reasons why it exists.

I find it supernatural that 2,000 years ago, in the Book of Revelation, John was shown a vision about today's society and modern technology. Billions of people worldwide are familiar with the Book of Revelation.

John the stenographer had been exiled to the island of Patmos so as not to be made a martyr by the Romans. While he was in exile, he was thrust forward in time and shown a vision concerning our time today, the end times. He was told to write down what he saw; the actual revelation was from Christ Himself. Revelation is a book in the Bible that's partly about money. Yes, it was also revealed at this point in time how we would be handling our finances today, a new and man-made type of buying and selling.

Many symbols, metaphors and prophecies in this final book were hidden in obscurity until the very end. This was substantiated when Christ told John to seal the book up until the end. I don't know how much more proof you need than that.

If you allow other books in the Bible to explain the revelation and you align it with today's technology, it is obvious that this book is of supernatural content. There are descriptions of modern warfare—tanks and flying machines that look like locusts with breastplates of iron. Apache attack helicopters, submarines, and aircraft were also described.

John must have been absolutely dazzled and scared to death after this revelation. He had been exposed only to the world that existed around him during this part of history, so his words were relevant to his time frame only.

Only after the next 2,000 years and after the Holy Bible had been canonized could we see how the modern world was explained in scriptures. Since this book is about the last generation and the end of recorded history as we know it, I can definitely attach it to our time frame. Only in today's world can we see the things that John described in ancient times.

John lived during the Roman Empire, where currency was used to buy and sell.. This basic way of buying and selling still exists today; the names of the currencies are different, but the process is identical. It's remarkably strange that a way of buying and selling with currencies has not changed in all history, but is about to shortly. The change began like never before: with the advent of the digital age and money-tracking capabilities.

The timeline and chronological order of events taking place in the world has set the stage for John's vision. For the last 50 years, mankind has been experimenting with more and different proficient ways to buy and sell. Some things we have adapted into our infrastructure are cryptocurrencies, credit cards and online purchasing. These are primitive forerunners of a man-made system that's about to occur. For now, it is still a system that's backed up and a part of a cash-based world.

Christ Himself said: "Render to Caesar the things that are Caesar's, and to God the things that are God's." This currency that America has used since its inception has the words "In God We Trust". There is a giant change about to take place at breakneck speed. This new man-made system requires you, as a participant, to be loyal and to swear an allegiance.

This new system will obviously be a man-centered way of doing business or, to say the least, it will be man's system and would have nothing to do with God. Just like we have taken God out of schools and out of our pledge of allegiance, our currency is next. We removed the ten commandments from buildings, universities and government to put distance between us and God, just to be politically correct.

Not only will our currency not endorse America's belief in God, it will not be allowed. Once again, you can thank the liberal press, politicians and political correctness for their part in removing God from your finances. Our current system is predicated and built on Christian values blessed and embraced by God Himself. To put God on your currency is a statement that says you trust Him more than you trust the currency itself. America's founders demanded this inscription on our currency.

But in a politically correct world, there are those who will not accept anything connected to God. There's a reason not to mention God: His word doesn't agree with the sexual rules we play by today, or our new allegiances.

There are many more Biblically unacceptable rules and paradigms of thinking that modern man has recently embraced. This is the reason why John was adamant in the Book of Revelation about not taking this mark that necessitates your allegiance. John was explaining that this last generation would not be interested in God, nor would they acknowledge Him for their prosperity.

The downside of this new system is that without your allegiance, cooperation, and compliance, you will not be able to buy even a loaf of bread. There will be many explanations and excuses that will be used to implement this new way of purchasing goods. According to scripture, this will be the final system in the final age of man's rule on this planet. This new system will involve numbers, as with all transactions; and of course, we have all heard that 666 will be the identifying trait.

There are many articles and books that speculate about the meaning of 666, but I surmise that the explanation is very simple. There is a dominant theme in the Bible concerning the number 6: that it is the number of man. According to Genesis, God engineered the world around man for 6 days, and the seventh day was called His day or the Sabbath. The general narrative in the Bible is that man will have 6,000 years to rule himself and make his own decisions, leaving God in or out of those decisions.

This is the reason why I believe 6 is connected to this monetary system. It is simply a reference or connected to being a man-made system. This man-made financial system will leave God out of the process and its decisions. Its goal will be to track every human being and every transaction, control your thought process and buying habits, and prohibit your religious freedom. Why would government want to prevent you from having religious freedom? The answer is simple: this new form of doing business wants full control, and will be designed by evil forces.

The drug epidemic in America has disarmed millions of sane minds that should be in this fight against evil. Instead of resisting, they will be compliant and willing participants.

Not only has the drug epidemic hurt us financially, internationally and domestically; it has also hurt us spiritually. Drugs will allow this new system to force you to deny and leave the great Creator out of your thinking. There are devious beings and minds that are poisoned by malevolent spirits that are after your eternity; drugs will make their job easier. We already know that drugs interfere with our logic, and of course we compromise our values. At the rate America is being addicted today, this new system will be easy to implement on a population of addicts. These addicts don't necessarily have to be on heroin or the needle; pharmaceuticals will also allow and ensure compliance.

In many opioid addicts, the desire for that drug can change the best character into weakness. A terrible wind of divisiveness now blows against our nation. We remember from history and even in elementary school that Abraham Lincoln said a nation divided cannot stand, and the nation united cannot fall.

Evil forces are now controlling the information that flows from your T.V. and social media into your mind as well as your children's minds. When a news anchor, editor, Facebook manager or anyone with influence delivers narratives to tens of millions, it can be dangerous. Turn on any channel; you will find liberals and conservatives both claiming the other is wrong. Since they are diametrically opposed, they can't both be right. It's your responsibility to define the truth, connect the dots, and examine both ways of thinking.

If there's anything suspicious about what you're hearing and seeing, if it is divisive and angers the masses, if it's subversive, it's probably wrong. This is creating animosity between the races, the haves and have-nots. To divide the races and the genders as well as different religious beliefs is Satanic in its very origins. This will divide our nation and create confusion, chaos, and pandemonium that will prevent us from surviving.

America doesn't have the same character and the same love or patriotism that we had in World War II. We are creating our own doubts about life, liberty, and America.

While watching the debates, I noticed that politicians will say literally anything to get elected. These are not people with the kind of character America can trust; they only want the power, the money, and the prestige. Once in office, most of these politicians use their power to get rich.

One of their most important tactics is to create animosity between different ethnicities and races at any cost, not really caring about anything but their own political race. This race-baiting has created a divided nation that will be easier for evil forces to influence. These evil forces want to disturb your peace and make you feel as if you're a victim in the past, present and future. They are good at instigation and subversion.

Now, let's get to the real nuts and bolts of this chapter. This chapter is so frightening, it scares even me. But we will tell the truth and point out the possibilities that could materialize in the modern global world that we all share. The world has become much smaller because of instant communication, extremely fast transportation, and the availability of so many new technologies. The stage is set for so many catastrophes and calamities to materialize that we as a people don't really need anyone to instigate, subvert or antagonize us against each other. The only reason we have survived thus far is because God was on our side, even more so than we were on His.

The second reason why America has persevered and overcome world wars, depressions, floods, hurricanes, and earthquakes is because we've always pulled together. Those who would perpetrate and instigate a lie know this, and this is the reason for their treason and subversion.

You don't have to look any further than your wallet or your bank account to understand and see everything that stands between you and your family's demise. Without any money, credit card, or some other form of payment, your family would be destitute with no safety or security. When you walk out of your home, you start your car and go to the closest convenience store for gas or a cup of coffee, and you need cash or a credit card for those things. We are never challenged on cash or credit cards if we have good credit.

We could have named this chapter "When Money Fails", but I prefer "If Money Fails" in hopes that our integrity and manufacturing base will always match the value of our currency. If you pick up cheeseburgers for lunch and you pay with a $20 bill, there is confidence from Burger King or McDonald's that cash is still good. This is why you leave with a cheeseburger, they get paper.

Our faith, belief and patriotism are the reasons why the entire world wants our currency. If you feel like you were mistreated at the convenience store because you couldn't pay for your gas or coffee with a credit card or cash, that could be laughable... If a real economic implosion happens. Imagine if, in America, no one's credit card was accepted anywhere.

But it could be many times worse than that: what if your cash was suddenly rendered worthless? So far, the entire world standard and world economies are based on the US dollar. This, of course, speaks volumes about how reliable American credit and business stability has been around the planet.

The fact that we are the gold standard and paper currency of the world speaks highly of our military because we offer security for banking freedom and investments around the planet. Most people don't equate it to that, nor do they make the connection that a strong military is the main reason we have a strong currency. What business or giant manufacturing organization would invest in an insecure nation, if their investment wasn't protected? The first reason of course we have a strong military: is the safety of our nation. It won't matter how secure, strong and powerful your military is if anything should ever happen to your currency. I say this because while your military is protecting you, our currency is protecting America's military.

This chapter makes me uncomfortable because I am treading in an area that is so fragile and delicate. Not only is it fragile, but it is also sensitive in its reactions to powerful words, conjecture, and a lack of faith.

America, look back at all great societies and their failed currencies. Ask yourself: Would you accept their money if you were selling merchandise? The answer would be a resounding no. America has proven over time that it can keep the American industry and monetary system on solid ground.

America, do not be naïve. If you think our enemies would not subvert, undermine and destroy our economic infrastructure, then you don't know modern warfare. The most precarious part of this new economic warfare is that we are globally integrated, and at a very dangerous and fragile level. Cyberattacks are hidden in the shadows, and are more powerful and dangerous than a nuclear weapon. Cyberwarfare has the capability to incapacitate an entire nation without ever firing a shot.

One such way that would incapacitate our entire economic infrastructure and render your money useless is electricity. America needs to address its electrical vulnerability because of our power grid. Our electric grid is connected to credit institutions and banking systems that account for almost every dollar, canceled check and transaction.

Our power grids are antiquated in many ways, but they're still the best in the world. America's power grid is the most vast yet the most vulnerable, and doesn't have any protective or defensive mechanisms. There is nothing built for our power grid to stop terrorism or any nation that can deliver an EMP.

For those who don't know what an EMP or electromagnetic pulse is, it is simply the energy wave caused by the detonation of an explosive device above the surface of Earth. This will have the same effect as a coronal mass ejection because of solar storms that land on Earth. To clarify, solar storms are a result of storms on the surface of the sun that create waves from outer space and can hit the Earth. Either or both of these can incapacitate and fry our exposed and fragile grids.

The power grid not only runs our economic infrastructure; it also runs all of our electronics. America has become dependent on everything from satellites in the sky to computers that spin out your lottery ticket or take your money for gas. You, as an American, can barely get your mind around what could happen without this grid no more than you can relate to the distances and objects across the universe.

Forget turning on your T.V., radio, cell phone, or anything thing that is electronic to get answers. If a terrorist or a recognized nation were to incapacitate our grid, you would not get treatment at the hospital. Backup generators would soon wear out and run out of fuel. Most generators would be incapacitated, like automobiles with sensitive computer components that could be destroyed by an EMP. If your car still runs, you would not be able to purchase gasoline, even if it were available.

Of course, forget groceries at Walmart or Kroger. Forget prescriptions, your blood pressure medicine, or paying your water bill. Everything from cash registers, meat supply houses, wholesale grocers and almost all trucks would cease to move within days.

There are many unknowns about the effectiveness of an EMP or a coronal mass ejection, but the general consensus is that the results would be far greater and maybe more devastating than a nuclear exchange. A recent survey and study concerning the devastation of an EMP attack revealed that 90% of America would die in a year.

On a side note, I find it ironic and a twist of destiny that third-world and agrarian societies would continue to live without much change. The reason for this is that they have not based their existence on a technological way of life. Most of these third-world nations catch their own fish and raise their own livestock, and are not dependent as much on electrical sources. Many of these nations are built around water, which means they don't always just turn on the tap. That is not to say they would not have millions of deaths, but the drop would not be as high as it would be for those living in civilized nations.

We grew up in America surrounded by electricity, and always took it for granted. We gripe when we get our electric bill or pay at the pump, and we're always looking for cheaper gas and electric bills. America, think of the consequences of not having an electric bill because there's no electricity to purchase. Any event of this magnitude could be the catalyst for us to consider a better way of doing business.

These fears, especially concerning the power grid, have produced a nation of hoarders, survivalists, and pessimists. If an EMP were to occur, this would facilitate a lack of confidence and faith in your currency. After all, what good is money if no one can open the cash register or if computers can't scan bar codes? Automobiles (mostly those made after 1990) would not run because an EMP would fry all sensitive electrical components. A type of panic never before seen by mankind would emerge and snowball. I say that it has never existed because never has there been this many millions in America alone who are so dependent on everything from computers to electricity.

I find it perplexing that our leaders whom we pay enormous salaries to haven't addressed this possibility. This is a real, proven possibility that has been acknowledged and delivered to Congress. Congress sees a government shutdown as the largest threat, one that will stop their paychecks.

When the power grid is knocked out during a hurricane, even if it happens in a large area, it's still considered a regional event. But power is usually restored in just a few days. With an EMP, we are in uncharted waters. We are not sure and there has not been a sufficient study to ascertain the consequences. This study could only guess about how long it would last.

Most electrical engineers who have presented their findings to Congress concur that it could last from two months to 10 years. This scenario would catapult America back 200 years without the capability to cope with 300 million untrained, unadapted and spoiled couch potatoes. If I appear harsh concerning the average American, it is only to wake them up and to expose this possibility.

At this point, would you want yourself or your loved ones on drugs and incapacitated if this happened?

A coronal mass ejection happened in the 1850s, knocking out telegraph communications. During this time in American history, we were not dependent on any of the technologies that we are reliant on today. America back then was more like Brazil or Mexico, or even parts of Asia today.

America's military has been more aware of this problem, and is quietly working behind the scenes to protect its capabilities electronically and offensively. This process caused by an EMP would also be affiliated and then facilitated by cyber hacking that would finish us off. You better hope and pray that our leaders have been zealous, aggressive and enthusiastic concerning the protection of our cyberinfrastructure. If our greatest minds cannot protect us militarily from cyber warfare, we should at least consider a backup system of pen and paper, for lack of a more simple terminology.

In World War II, an estimated 70 million human beings perished. If money and currency were to fail, it is estimated that as many as 200 million Americans alone could die. As you read this, there are men and women sitting in think tanks in different countries, plotting and planning your death through economic subversion. These people, these enemies of America are adamant about using these techniques to bring about your demise.

Trade wars can be the beginnings of shooting wars, and were the cause of war between America and Japan in 1941. The possibility of trade wars happening very swiftly today are enormous, and they have actually begun. Most Americans want to avoid a trade war at any cost, but that cost is part of this $21 trillion deficit.

For those who are missing the facts like the liberal fake news channels, I have news for you. These trade agreements, many of which are antiquated and date back to the end of World War II, favored other nations so as to allow them to get back on their feet at the end of that war.

The same nations that are complaining about recently implemented tariffs should know that they should have been in play 30 years ago. No longer at war, many of them are now better off financially than we are in America, yet we still pay the lion's share for their defense. Their argument is they fought by our side and helped us defeat the Axis powers in World War II. That is true, but that is only half of the story because we also fought by their side and they would be speaking German or Japanese and living under dictatorship if we had not done so.

In the case of one rival, China, as its economy booms and it becomes successful, it needs more resources, real estate, petroleum, food and everything else to sustain a working and growing population. Expansion in real estate, geography and population is what fuels nations like China once they emerge as economic giants.

It is also true that a growing population must be dedicated, loyal and patriotic to the government of that country, no matter their belief system. China and Russia have had a love-hate, hot-and-cold, ambivalent relationship, which always influences America one way or the other. Of course, when this happens, China has no interest in seeing America clean and sober; it prefers an opiate-addicted America.

China is one nation that has seen the results of opiate addiction. It has been a curse for the Far East more than Western nations. The poppy plant is indigenous to countries like China and Afghanistan. The Opium Wars and all mixtures derived from the poppy plant have been responsible for destroying the economic infrastructure of China for centuries. This one drug is the reason why they have not already conquered the entire world. This knowledge of how poppy plants can bring down a nation is China's most powerful weapon. China also knows the consequences on America because of pharmaceutical opiates.

Muslim nations have introduced powerful amounts of black tar heroin into our streets. These players are partners in crime, and the middleman who did most of their delivery has been Mexico. I try and I want to love the Mexican people; they are decent and humane people. But drugs have produced bad results. That's usually because of corrupt government officials; but on an individual basis, the desire for money has defeated good character concerning drugs. The corruption involved in the delivery of opiates across our southern border and around the planet is far greater than ever before.

China is very much in bed with a large pharmaceutical industry that permeates every square block and citizen in the United States. This industry pushes an enormous amount of synthetic pain pills into our medical system. Its alignment with the pharmaceutical industry is very bad and subversive. Its intentions are to undermine our heritage, weaken our infrastructure, and incapacitate 40% of our nation.

At this point, China is very aware that tangling with America on the high seas would be genocide on their part. Our navy is superior in almost every category, if not all. To launch an attack on the United States on the high seas would be futile and suicidal.

This is why nations like China are using a slow, methodical way to incapacitate, demoralize and subvert our economy and currency. Almost once a month, you hear of a breach in our banking and credit card systems, with cyber hacking done by China or Russia. These opposing superpowers are prodding and testing the waters for the big one. We must invent, reinvent, and think outside the box to head off and beat them mentally as well as in a shooting war.

To neutralize our economic infrastructure would be a form of decapitation, destroying our morale and causing us to surrender without a fight. America has the greatest military on Earth, but it is in jeopardy of being compromised by cyberwarfare.

China now has the capability and weapons in place to shoot down or destroy satellites in orbit. There has also been an aggressive move by China as well as other foreign leaders to topple the dollar as the world standard. There are other players standing in line if America falls. Europe and the European Common Market formed one currency 35 years ago. This was prophesied thousands of years ago, and it happened. China is trying to accomplish this today.

When the European Common Market was born and the Euro was accepted, it was actually an attempt to overcome the dollar. Great Britain will probably drop out of the EU, and it was Biblically prophesied to do just that.

There is nothing wrong with world trade. It allows nations access to goods and services that are not produced in and within their own borders. The problem occurs when people, leaders and nations get wealthy; and they want an unbalanced amount of power to control pricing. This is what happens when the world becomes globalist and there are no options. Yes, even global trade and principles are explained in Biblical scriptures.

We all know that liberals prefer a world with no borders, no privacy, and no sovereignty; yet they claim they prefer equal wealth for everyone. It's when you try to take back what has been stolen from you that there is a problem. This is why the world is resisting Donald Trump. This is why American wealth and sovereignty must remain: it's as much a possession as your family.

Without being too political, our last election was almost destroyed by a media that was financed and influenced by globalists. These elites are determined to destroy America's sovereignty. If it appears that I am anti-liberal, that is not true. I would love to be a liberal without taking away the incentive to make your own way. When you destroy sovereignty, you destroy the ability to own a country and your dignity. To give away another man's wealth for votes is tantamount to treason, and is a model of third-world dictatorships. This is the reason for relaxed immigration policies fueled and composed by the Democratic Party.

It appears they have decided they would give away everything from the Lincoln Monument to our national treasure to immigrants as long as they vote democratic. This technique is not earning your vote; it is buying your vote, regardless of the kind of leader you would be. These immigrants are told to always vote Democrats, and most do. It gets worse. It isn't even about buying votes with their money; it's about buying votes with someone else's money: the taxpayer.

America was founded on the hope that someday, you will prosper beyond your wildest dreams. This dream—to live free in a land where you can come and go—is called freedom. This plan to undo our borders has been facilitated, and the grease the globalists have used in abundance are drugs and welfare.

This ingredient of sovereignty is not a part of globalist requirements. In fact, the Democratic Party has declared sovereignty a roadblock for globalization. If ever America is no longer the leading world power and we have no sovereignty, it will never be replaced by a nation that will protect you or your descendants again.

We talked at the beginning of this chapter about the failure of our currency. America, the only way a new world order can take place and be accepted is for the globalists to first destroy the existing system. As catastrophic as that would be, it would open the door for a new monetary system that was prophesied thousands of years ago.

As identity theft and cyber activity grow with money laundering and counterfeit currencies, millions will look for alternatives. Faith in our existing system will collapse as this happens; the average person, when desperate, would be more accepting and compliant.

There are already economic think tanks working 24/7 to bring about a new way of buying and selling. This is one of the reasons why your buying habits, preferences and algorithms are constantly being studied. Most think it's about selling products, but it's more or as much about how you buy than what you buy.

What I know to be true as prophecy just a few years ago has now come to fruition. There are new databases containing everything about your criminal records, medical history, voting patterns, and even the type of T.V. programs you view. Your food preferences and anything and everything from your DNA, eye color, sexual habits, and religious and marital status are all now available. The risk of credit card and identity theft along with counterfeit money will get so bad, it will be one of the excuses for this system.

All of these reasons will facilitate and promote this new way of buying and doing business. During the first couple years of transition, there will be confusion as America is acclimated until it becomes irreversible. We will be forced into this new system, along with the rest of the world. At this point, the liberal press, the globalists, and those who want open borders will celebrate because they will know it is irreversible. These brainwashed millions will know that America as a sovereign nation is no more.

Confusion won't come immediately in the new system pointed out in the Book of Revelation. This new system will appear to work seamlessly. Billions will accept it worldwide, unaware of what's behind it. This worldwide system, identified as the mark of the beast, will have a short lifespan paralleled by man-made and natural calamities never before seen on Earth.

This new system will necessitate your allegiance and cooperation. It most likely will not be an implanted microchip. Microchipping will not be used for the monetary part of this system; it will be used as a tracking system to facilitate control over the Earth's billions.

I know that this microchip is a big favorite with a lot of scholars, but the truth is that this system will be even more simple because all it will necessitate is a simple scan of your eyes, face or your fingerprints. No two sets of irises or fingerprints are alike.

Our DNA will not have to deal with the rejection of a microchip or the possibility of it being stolen and duplicated. Fundamental science knows that if someone steals your arm or your eye, their bodies will reject it because it will not be compatible. In a practical term, it appears that this would be a more proficient and less stressful way of purchasing a pack of cigarettes, a loaf of bread, or a new Mercedes.

In all actuality, let's surmise that a scan of your iris and your fingerprint will be facilitated and backed up by a chip that will report your whereabouts. Of course, what you buy and where you buy will immediately provide a travel and location history within seconds. Satellites will be the vehicle to inform databases (via the microchip) of your whereabouts as a matter of redundancy. In other words, your purchase and location and the type of business you are conducting will be in this database. Only recently has this capability been available with the advent of nanotechnology. It's available and waiting to be infrastructured into a worldwide system controlled by the globalists.

This is chronologically the time frame that will work in alignment with the Book of Revelation, as recorded by John. This, of course, is also proof of the Biblical prophecy that could have never materialized even 20 years ago.

Keep in mind that everything we have just itemized is a man-made system. If you pull a dollar bill out of your wallet and read the words "In God We Trust", those words will not be integrated into this new system. This is because our original monetary system, founded by our forefathers, was predicated and endorsed by God Himself. The recognition that this country was a blessing from God is the difference. This is also why America has been blessed and seen miracles in her wars since its beginning. Our character was also structured around Biblical principles that we have morphed away from.

The stage is set. Any number of incidents or scenarios can bring about this new world order and render American currency—and perhaps all other currencies—null and void in a very short time. These powerful globalists and individuals, who are a part of creating a new world order, share the same goals that have been handed down for generations. Only now have all the ingredients and all of the circumstances and scenarios come together in a perfect storm at the exact time they were prophesied to occur. These goals are to achieve a world in which the masses will be subservient to just a few.

Governments will be able to maintain strict taxes with no cheating or discrepancies because nothing will be bought with cash. Money laundering by drug dealers will no longer exist; there will be many reasons that will fuel this change. One other logic that will be pushed by proponents of a cashless culture will be germs from money passed by hand because of prior epidemics. All of this logic, including identity theft, will make sense to the masses; but won't be the truth, reason or motive for this new system. The truth is drug dealers, con artists, and white-collar criminals will maneuver around the system and get their payment in some other way.

Also, the objective will be to implement one world religion because if the population is all on the same page, it creates complacency. Prior to this happening, there will of course be a couple of stormy years to indoctrinate your mind to accept this change.

This entire paradigm, this technology is about giving the powers-that-be every aspect and control of your existence. The masses will become subservient and conform to their rules. That's a loss of your personal sovereignty; by now, your national sovereignty would be long gone. Once this system is complete and you have become dependent on it for your very survival, these powers will consider you no more than mindless worker ants. The dark side of their agenda won't be realized and exposed until it's irreversible.

Most Americans don't realize that at the beginning of every calendar year, there are hundreds (if not thousands) of new laws passed during the previous year that become active. These new laws will increase in their ability to take away your privacy and your ability to decide for yourself, in pretty much the same way the globalists and the liberal press are eating away at our borders. These laws are being passed and will be implemented quietly in the night. It will be the slow but steady acceptance of these new laws that would be the strategy making people think they are not worth fighting over.

You will be innocent in your thinking, but remember the Jews pre-World War II. Remember how they continued to accept one act after another perpetrated on them by the Nazi regime until over 6 million were murdered and millions more were enslaved?

The science and the exact method of this new monetary system are not as important as the consequences. In all fairness, whether it is an iris scan or a fingerprint scan or even a microchip, the results will be the same. The only difference is the technique that will be used to procured your personal data would then implement this system.

Law enforcement, government agencies, medical facilities, and local jurisdictions worldwide will have access to your database. Once you have committed what they will consider even a small infraction, they will have an opening to snoop around. We said earlier that the technology is already in play to watch you while you're watching T.V. Drones, satellites, any all aerial and land surveillance cameras (even street lights) are now watching you and documenting your every move. This system is evolving alongside increased technical advances and nanotechnologies that will soon be married.

Keep in mind that the world you are seeing from your window right now is actually quiet, peaceful and stable. But this stability and peace is more fragile than you can ever imagine. In this country, it's now possible for a race war and revolution to occur and weaken us internally.

 At the same time, the black populations in Chicago, Dallas and other major cities throughout America are dying in greater numbers than ever before. This has only fueled the drug epidemic because blacks are as much a victim as any other race, maybe more as a result of geopolitics.

After the last 20 years with a type of mental perception by black Americans, they feel intimidated and threatened. To let young black males die on the streets while their mothers cry isn't what great black leaders intended.

I realize that as a reader, if you are black and you are reading this, it is hard to change your assumptions. The truth is that drugs have been allowed to flow unabated to every city in America, bringing death, guns and blood to black America like never before. A race war in America could materialize as a result of the social brainwashing that will be embraced by globalists.

If you are black and you are reading this, look at history. Look how Hitler convinced the German population how they had been wronged and that the Jews were the cause of all their economic problems. We now know that this was wrong. It left Germany in ashes, and its place in history will forever be tarnished during that time in history.

I think it's only right that I interject this: the truth is that almost no white man can look at the world through the historical lens and eyes of any black American. You, as a black American, should also know once this new system is in place, racial equality will be the smallest threat to you or your white counterparts.

This book isn't about slavery, but all of mankind can possibly be enslaved by this epidemic if the truth is not exposed. This enslavement won't be traditional slavery; it will be implemented slowly like the drug epidemic so as not to alert us.

To black and white America, the window to unite our nation is closing. Once this demonic system has been implemented, black, white and all other ethnicities, cultures and races will no longer have the opportunity to fight side by side to overcome it. Then we will all suffer together.

There is a sinister reason to create a cashless society. With this new system, you will not be able to buy or sell without giving up your whereabouts, so there's no escape. As we said earlier, one excuse would be clinical germs as newer and stronger epidemics kill millions.

There is already a confluence and collusion of these two sciences that are at work watching, listening and observing, even as you read this book. Their main objective is not your health or your finances; it is control of your sovereignty, your habits and your loyalty. Even your thought process is their ultimate goal. To control your thinking will prevent insurrection and resistance of the masses, making us more compliant.

As fake news pushes more racial divides, its objective is to make you spend more time thinking about words than thinking about logic. The main news channel that was trusted for decades is obsessed with the overthrow of America. These news channels care only about racial divide to further a globalist world.

The potential to control every human being on Earth is the objective in the modern world, and will soon exist. The only people who will be impervious to this control will live in an agrarian or obscured place. Mind-control drugs that are being pushed by the medical field will make this possible.

The type of behavior that permeates our land and our nation today would not have been accepted 40 years ago. It seems the drug epidemic coupled with the new Hollywood has changed our morals. The hint of pedophilia is nationwide: a gay person or transgressions are to be accepted. If you challenge it, you could be prosecuted or sued. Will pedophilia soon have that same consequence and status? Remember that only a few decades ago, gay relationships were illegal in most states. Will there come a time when you will be forced to accept pedophilia or be prosecuted?

A large percentage of America's population now doesn't even think that defending our country and our freedoms is worth it. We now have a generation of young people who are considering alternative forms of social structures and governments. Apparently, socialism always materializes in a society that has had it too easy for too long, and with too much time on their hands.

Drugs have certainly played a role in this thinking. I'm sorry, but I'm going to make a lot of people mad with this next statement. It appears that when same-sex marriage materialized and was legalized, we made God mad. That might sound like a simple statement, but sometimes right and wrong aren't that complicated. Our sexual preferences changed from what would have been a jail sentence in the '60s to a marriage license and shared Social Security benefits today.

Drugs have changed us to a large percentage, with no ambition, no drive, and no morals. No, I'm not implicating our entire population. But the masses would have never accepted same-sex marriage a couple of decades ago.

Strangely, another thing that has changed is the number of doctors who write prescriptions. Doctors are all living in mansions even with their mediocre practices, while our people are strung out on opiates like never before. These opiates are so powerful, you could do brain surgery while patients are under the influence without putting them to sleep.

Yes, there is a connection between powerful narcotics and the acceptance of sexual morals. Ask anyone who was molested as a child. Most would certainly tell you it was while the perpetrators were either on meth, coke or prescription drugs.

If you are gay and you espouse to marry someone of the same gender, you will hate me at this point. I am sorry, but I must tell the truth and explain what has helped to facilitate this change in our country.

The one giant leap with gay and lesbian couples recently was to bring God into their relationships. You cannot marry anyone of the opposite sex or the same sex without invoking the name of God because it is an institution created by God. When I say they brought God to their marriage, it was to give credibility to a marriage that is adamantly forbidden. You can't change His scriptures the same way many have changed their genders. They are the same today as yesterday, and always will be.

I'm not trying to demonize the LGBT movement, but no law voted in by a liberal agenda trumps or supersedes God's word. This same logic that pushed powerful narcotics has produced same-sex marriage. Once again, this liberal logic that has tried to change scripture is trying to make us a nation of socialists and welfare recipients, incapacitated and compliant.

There is also a proven fact that America's homeless society is 600% greater today than 40 years ago. The homeless are not like this because of the difference in the haves and have-nots. No, they are homeless as a result of open borders and drug use. You cannot deny that in almost every small and large town, the numbers of young and able-bodied Americans holding signs looking for a handout have increased. These signs will read anything from "will work for food" to as something simple as "down on my luck".

The very first thing you'll think when you pass a homeless person with a sign is they need a bath. Next would be that they need a job, and then a bath. I guarantee that the other thought in your mind is they're on drugs. Sadly, you will be right. When the drug epidemic is defeated, these young Americans won't be sleeping in the rain because they can't pass a drug test; they will own homes. These Americans living under bridges will once again have dignity, jobs and better health.

These drugs will make you give up your personal sovereignty. What is that? Your personal sovereignty is the right to own yourself, to think and to choose your religious path, and to make choices that you deserve. It is you looking into the mirror of freedom.

The liberals want you to think that our old way of thinking, which has gotten us through many wars, will not work in today's world. Therefore, your private sovereignty is the first casualty. After your sovereignty is gone, all other rights and dignities will be relegated and given to you on an as-needed basis.

If this sounds like some far-fetched movie or scenario for futuristic worlds, it is happening now. Of course, it won't stop there: total control of your thinking process is their goal. This logic and motive is the reason why the drug war has continued for 60 years in America. The globalists and the elitists began influencing our political thinking with a devious outcome in mind decades ago.

Of course, we all lose our sovereignty if we were arrested and sent to prison or jail as a result of drugs. If China, Russia, the Islamic world or Europe succeeds in replacing America on the world stage, it will be because our character and sobriety have failed.

Many scenarios can bring America to third-world status almost overnight. If you think nations in Europe, Asia or any third-world country would not capitalize on our bad luck, then you better grow up.

I'll give you a couple of scenarios. One is a giant caldera that exists in the middle of America called Yellowstone. According to historical research, Yellowstone erupts every six hundred thousand years, give or take a few decades. This caldera or supervolcano can turn America into an ashtray overnight. The amount of ash, plume and fire would render 70% of America's farming capability useless in just a couple of days. This volcano has erupted many times, and volcanologists are aware that it is overdue.

Not only is it overdue, but geyser and seismic activity are more prevalent today than only a few short years ago. It is at the edge of or a part of the Pacific Ring of Fire, and so is the Hawaiian volcano that convulsed for months in 2018. Unlike protecting our power grid or negotiating a peace treaty over nuclear weapons, there is no power on this planet to stop its destruction.

A nuclear winter would also ensure that the entire planet and other nations would suffer as well, but not as much as America. Not only would we suffer the consequences, pandemonium would cause all infrastructure and monetary infrastructure to be useless and worthless in days.

America also has numerous nuclear power plants that could be destroyed as a result of this volcano, with no time to shut down the reactors. A sudden event like a Yellowstone eruption could do damage that's similar to what we saw at the Fukushima nuclear plant in Japan.

All of these events (and there are more) would cause zero confidence in the dollar.

The real problem with America is we don't believe in ourselves anymore. Political correctness has placed handcuffs our leaders, with too many chiefs and no Indians. It seems that the inability to please every ethnicity, race and culture each time a decision is made can destroy us quicker than war. It is obvious that the liberal left has caused confusion because of political correctness designed to hamstring our nation.

Epidemics and pandemics have the capability now of spreading so fast that if the right one gets enough clutch, it could be even more devastating than Yellowstone. America has the best medical facilities in the world, but we're clinically less resilient to epidemics because we have overprescribed antibiotics. America is intoxicated on a cocktail of pharmaceutical drugs that suddenly will not be available.

Some of these catastrophes can kill so many, there won't be enough living people to bury the dead. Burying the dead would not even be our biggest problem; those would be starvation and (the number-one necessity that will be the hardest to find) clean drinking water.

Other world players like China and Russia lie in wait in case any of these natural catastrophes should happen to us. If America was brought down by a naturally occurring calamity, there would be no one to seek for retaliation. Believe it or not, there are conspiracy theories and even intelligent people who feel that enemy nations can control weather and seismic activity.

There are many who ask how China became almost equal to America and, in some ways, surpassed us in only a few years. It has been neck and neck with America in science technology, space exploration and, most importantly, military capabilities. When Richard Nixon open the door to China in the '70s, he unwittingly unleashed a sleeping giant of economic superiority.

The reason why China is so successful is because it is hungry; and America was fat, lazy, and complacent during the '70s, much like today. Nixon's motives were good; and in some ways, these have produced good consequences. When China realized in the '70s that it would have access to unfettered markets in America, all it had to do utilize the masses; and this, it had plenty of. American workers could not compete with Chinese workers who were starving and willing to work for just a fraction of the profit that we enjoyed.

America's bad work ethic during the '70s was created by a nation zoned out on street drugs, especially pot. Pharmaceutical drugs that you will find at almost every home in America today are now assisting China. China was very aware that the average American was more interested in what day of the week they had to go to work, and when they could take off. It knew labor unions were forcing businesses to pay more in wages that produced less quantities and poor quality from the average worker. China also knew about the effects of marijuana, and its effects in the world of manufacturing. This nation with a plentiful source of labor was impossible to compete with, especially if your workers were stoned like in the '70s. These starving millions of Chinese created a perfect storm for America to lose its manufacturing base.

As manufacturing moved out of America and our drug epidemic got worse, it became irreversible. China took advantage of America's naïve complacency and distracted attitude of entitlement for many different reasons. The Chinese soon began to steal prototype technologies from our industries. It didn't stop there; they purchased then simply reverse-engineered our products, then reproduced them at half the price.

Espionage and white-collar treason by some Americans have assisted this theft by China. The Chinese are now hacking into every category of banking and economic infrastructure that America has with a plan. Its plan is simple: when a shooting war happens with America, they will attack all our cyber-capabilities. These news reports that we see occurring weekly about cyberhacking are just war games they are practicing.

Mexico was the first to realize how easy America's workforce was to incapacitate. Because of its close proximity, it was easy to send in a cheaper labor force. But first, the drugs must enter the U.S. Economic subversions are easily created in a world where populations become larger and larger.

As humans live closer and closer together, germs are unleashed onto a world that has no immunity. The first place we go to in case of serious sickness, trauma or any ailment is the emergency room. America's emergency rooms are good in treating all types of trauma, viruses or excessive bleeding—and of course, overdoses.

Along with many of these patients comes a very resistant strain of staph infection (MRSA) usually associated with meth users and needle use. This is a byproduct of treating these individuals that puts you, a non-user, at risk every time you go to a hospital. The one place you go to save your life can be the riskiest you have to enter. These hardened microbes continue to evolve and re-adapt to our latest lines of antibiotics.

To those of you who think these scenarios we listed are not likely to happen, know this: they are already occurring. These new modern-day horrors were accurately prophesied thousands of years ago.

Once you study the chronology of events that were identified, itemized and then foretold, you will see the proof with your own eyes. When you turn on the news, you are witnessing a Biblical truth foretold centuries ago. Biblical scriptures may sound preposterous in a modern world, but now is the time to take them seriously.

More than ever before, it is time to look with an intelligent mind and really ask yourself: Could this really be happening as prophesied?

I want you, as an audience and as a reader, to know I am not affiliated with any church or denomination. However, seeing this much proof and not believing it would be the equivalent of believing there's no Arizona. I hope you appreciate that I am not trying to garner a donation, nor am I trying to recruit you as a member of any organization. I am a believer by faith, backed up by intelligence. Therefore, I could never deny proof that's in my face.

You are welcome to draw your own conclusions; your faith is not what I am trying to enlist. This work is only intended to save lives, and explain and expose to America and your family an epidemic. I have pointed out scriptures that existed 2,000 years ago because they accurately described current world events that cannot be denied. The benefit of reading and protecting your family with this work is for every person, with or without a theological, spiritual, or Biblical application.

If you can point me to any other documents or book with such accuracy, I will read it, evaluate it, and take it seriously. I surmise that this will not happen because when one reads the accuracy of current events, there is no denying the Bible's authenticity. You don't have to take my word for this, but it would be an interesting journey for you to prove or disprove these historical accounts written thousands of years ago.

In a strange twist, the war on drugs has been capitalized on to confiscate your cash, spy on you, and remove your right to privacy. This will get worse, and has given our government the power to spy in the drug war. It is considered a part of our security and a penalty or price we are expected to pay for our safety because of terrorism and drugs. In some ways, this intrusion and theft of our privacy has become more of a threat than the actual war on drugs itself.

One consequence of the drug war is that it has forced law enforcement to shoot thousands of young people on the streets. I find it strange and perplexing that 20% of our nation is under indictment or imprisoned for something that could have been stopped at our borders. Drugs have been allowed to flourish and thrive, creating a giant industry in the judicial field.

This industry that is guarding America is comprised of security data and medical and background checks on almost every American. Also, illegal automobile searches, wiretaps, and confiscation of cash quite often occur to the innocent. The heavy-handedness and overreach of law enforcement in many cases is similar to the gestapo in World War II-era Germany. We have locked ourselves in our homes, creating a self-imposed prison, and making it unclear if we are locked in or if the bad guys are locked out. Either way, we lose our freedom.

Hold on, it gets worse. The war on terrorism has become a war on your sovereignty and your privacy, in the same way the drug war has done.

This is the reason I have aligned myself with President Trump in preventing terrorists from coming to America, either legally or through illegal immigration. The previous administrations set the bar so low for immigration from terrorist nations, it became dangerous for our country.

This war on terrorism has had the same thinking that the war on drugs has. Our previous leaders have been very careful not to say that we are at war with Islam in America because it's a religion. I won't sugarcoat it: Islamist extremists and thousands of American soldiers and people around the planet have died because of their so-called religion. Make no mistake, America: we may not be at war with these extremists; but don't kid yourself, they're at war with us.

If we call this ideology a religion, we will have to take another look at Hitler and the Third Reich. America was founded on the freedom of religion. No matter if it's Baptist, Pentecostal, Protestant, Catholic or Islamist—it must not be the religion of subversion or anarchy. President Dwight D. Eisenhower said that "Freedom of worship is great, but it's not a right to destroy the Bill of Rights."

Since Donald Trump has basically destroyed ISIS, we appear to be winning the war on terrorism. This is because he called it for what it was: Islamic terrorism.

The drug war and the terrorist war are much more connected than you, the average American, can imagine. The Islamic world realizes the devastation delivered to America by the sale of drugs. Money generated by the sale of heroin on the streets of America has helped finance ISIS and many other terrorists' attacks.

One might ask why there is such beef between Western Christianity and the Islamic world, and why it has accelerated within the last 60 years. The answer to these questions may surprise you. This war has existed since the time of ancient Israel, Abraham, Isaac and Jacob.

The one doctrine that the Koran is very adamant about is killing those who are not of the same belief. Why it went dormant for a thousand years and resurfaced in the last 60 years is simple: oil. It wasn't that the animosity and the desire to kill weren't there; it was because they didn't have the money until the sale of oil.

Don't be so naïve, America. The love affair that the Islamic world has with us is based on money and Western technology. For the last 50 years, the Western world and China have furnished the money for Islamists to terrorize. Their hatred of Israel and the Covenant that they feel like they were cheated out of by Abraham have been their reasons to kill.

Now, through opiates from Afghanistan, the Islamic world has supplied the world with 74% of its heroin. When an American dies of a heroin overdose, a terrorist has killed an American just as much as on the battlefield. Also, many Americans kill other Americans while on heroin produced by the Islamists in Afghanistan.

This is the reason why Donald Trump promised severe vetting and deportation for those with any connection to drugs or terrorism. What is so perplexing for me and many Americans is why so many other Americans have resisted his efforts. It appears they don't read the papers, and look in the obituaries or into the eyes of the young people who have lost their battle with heroin.

There is an old saying that you cannot sell from an empty shelf. If they can't get drugs across our border, they can't sell to our kids.

We mentioned earlier that you can control whether or not you do drugs. We have also proven that you cannot control the availability of drugs. This process that Mr. Trump is pushing will be successful in preventing availability. President Trump's process against illegal immigration, terrorism, and illicit street drugs is the only real solution. Sadly, it will not have a great effect on pharmaceuticals, but it's the best effort I have witnessed in my life regarding street drugs.

Truthfully, it might make the problem worse for some. Many of you may wonder how it could get worse. But it can. The truth is that when heroin has dried up on the streets, many people will turn to pharmaceutical drugs for the same results. Strangely, if the coin is flipped, many who are on prescription-based opiates will turn to heroin if the pharmaceutical source is stopped. That's why the problem has to be attacked simultaneously on two fronts.

Whether or not any or all of these tragedies fall upon our nation, one thing is for certain. Being clean and sober will allow you a better chance of survival.

Let's just surmise that none of these calamities or catastrophes will ever materialize. It would still be great for you to live your life and enjoy the greatest nation with the greatest freedom; and to raise your children without the pain, suffering, and loss caused by this epidemic.

In closing this chapter, I would like to mention and commend those who would try to save their loved ones. The fight can be almost a death sentence to you; but if you lose and they die, you will have a little piece of mind and sanity knowing you fought the good fight. For years after their death, if you didn't try, you'd always feel you could have done more.

We all have our different ways of coping and fighting to bring about a good result. Know this: you will get well and over the stress and the financial losses. The one thing you will never get back is another chance to put that child back on the right track.

Chapter 8

Spiritual Consequences

For some of my readers, this may be the most intriguing, fascinating, and controversial chapter in this or any other book.

If there really is a spiritual war of good and evil occurring and you are a pawn, what better way to give the enemy leverage than drugs? Drugs produce results that make you a pawn that's easily seduced, distracted, and oblivious to reality. Drugs can entice you to do the things that are contrary to the laws of nature and physics.

Characteristics that produce death, destruction, incarceration, poor health, and a short lifespan will be the force that will be explained here. As a free moral agent, you have the right to decide which way or path to go. The reason you are offered this right is actually very simple: if you were forced to do right, it would be impossible to develop good character.

This is why you must be guided by a spirit that doesn't make you do right, but encourages you to and actually tells you when you're wrong. This requires a supernatural, invisible entity that convicts and reveals to you when you're doing right or wrong.

When man follows his own logic and is influenced by drugs, there is even more interference in the natural flow of good that renders guilt or consciousness ineffective. I am not saying that man is inherently evil; but for the most part, human nature in itself is carnal and produces selfish results. Drugs can allow you to murder your neighbor; steal his lawnmower, his identity and credit cards; or burn his house down to open a Pandora's box of evil.

In America, we now have an entire generation of young people who have been exposed to one form of drugs or another. There's also an immense interest now in Satanism, witchcraft, and the occult. Look at many of our young people. You will notice an inordinate aura of negativity surrounded by spiritual unknowns.

Yes, I know young people always dress differently just to defy the establishment. I'm not talking about the teenager who won't mow the lawn and wants everything handed to him while he watches T.V. from the couch. I am talking about an entire generation that has had access from everything to Ritalin and bath salts or pain pills from prescriptions or their parents' medicine cabinet.

One of the major fake news networks who are trying to take away your Second Amendment rights did a survey. According to their sources, which are never named, no other nation has shootings like America. Instead of identifying drugs or violent videos, they always point to gun control. This same network failed to mention that Mexico, which has the highest drug population, also has the largest murder-by-gun population.

It doesn't stop there. Newer and stronger strains of marijuana, synthetic drugs and other street drugs are being used by this generation. If you go fishing or to church, Walmart or Dairy Queen when you walk outside your door, it's a more dangerous world because of these changes.

The influence of Satanism and bizarre, violent and sadistic horror films along with every accessible internet video has created a culture that we have never experienced. It's no secret that Hollywood not only endorses but embraces and welcomes Satanic objectives. It is almost a requirement now that you be aligned with this type of belief system to be a successful actor.

This weird and dangerous culture that has emerged leads to a generation with almost no moral compass. We already know that when someone has no feelings of pain and suffering inflicted upon others coupled with drug use, you have the perfect storm. It's now children killing parents and committing school shootings as well as other bizarre rituals.

The most famous school shooting in America is Columbine. It comes to mind when we talk about supernatural influences on young minds. The shooter asked Cassie René Bernall if she believed in God as she hid under a table. She immediately answered yes, and he shot her. This young girl's courage should give every American goosebumps and inspiration at the same time.

America, how much more evidence do you need that this is spiritual warfare? If school shootings and bullying aren't enough, there's more. Many of these same children have been victimized by older relatives or acquaintances through pedophilia and sexual perversion. In most (if not all) cases, drugs were a part of this evil in one capacity or another.

The number of parents killing their children is at an all-time high. While the parents of these children were both working to ascertain materialism, their most important possession was in danger. What may be worse is that many parents don't even consider their children precious anymore.

In many instances, drugs can and have made the human mind malleable and twisted for the purpose of evil. This is also the reason why drug users who commit crime have no guilt. Coupled with demonic activity, the drug epidemic in our nation has breached the barriers of human logic.

As humans, we are unbelievably unique that most have no idea how important we are in the universe. NASA hasn't found anything else as unique and intelligent as human beings in the cosmos so far. If there is anything in the universe as important as you and as aware of its existence, it will also be attacked by these evil forces. This battle of good versus evil is just as prevalent in the cosmos as matter versus antimatter, and are opposing forces.

These two forces are as diametrically opposite as the north end and the south end of a magnet. They are just as opposite as love versus hate, death versus life... I think you get the picture.

It is important that you realize one thing: you are millions of times more important than you've ever realized. Of course, this begs the question of why you are important. It's because in many theological circles, it is believed that God is reproducing a form of Himself in you, just like how you reproduce yourself when you have a child; it is a thousand times greater in love and meaning when God produced you. It is obvious that you are the greatest thing that God has His eyes on here on Earth. It is also obvious, according to scripture, that His love for you is as awesome as the universe itself.

It's also the reason why you're a target. Your human potential, good or bad, is available and recorded until you die; then it becomes your legacy. After you die, the only thing that you will take with you will be your character. Your eternal potential is dependent upon your behavior while here on Earth. This character is challenged and influenced when you are subjected to the forces of physics. The decisions made by your character either produce good or bad results and consequences. We know that throughout history, individuals with bad character have made decisions that have cost millions of lives.

You may be asking yourself why you are being put through this test. If you believe in the scriptures, then you have read about a great galactic battle or insurrection in the heavens. This war of rebellion was caused by Lucifer's decision to try to overthrow the God Family. I am of the belief that he was not tested, nor were the angels assisting him tested in this three-dimensional environment that you are subjected to every day. We know they obviously had the ability to go either way and to rebel because some did. We also know from the scriptures that the angels are lower in importance than man is to God. From the scriptures, they appear to be spirit beings not subject to the same laws of physics that you must fight every day.

I am not saying dogmatically that they were not tested; I am saying that I see no scriptures that point to them being subject to the laws of physics like man. Since I don't know the secrets of the universe, I can only surmise; and this is not to claim adamantly there were no test or rewards.

Conjecture concerning Biblical unknowns must be looked at in the same way we view hypothetical science. The only way to discuss them is with interest and uncertainties. Angels may or may not have the same rights that you do concerning their decisions. The question is: Are they subject to the laws of gravity, an empty stomach, or the desire to sleep with someone's wife? The Book of Enoch seems to suggest that the fallen angels may have mated with Earth women prior to the flood. This book isn't about the hierarchy concerning angels; I'm sure they have a great purpose, and all evidence suggest they protect us.

You, a more important creation, are being tested by drugs designed by man himself that can make you fail this test. If you pass this test while subjected to a three-dimensional existence, it will be easy to trust you once you are no longer subjected to the laws of physics. Once you make the transformation from physical to spiritual, the laws of physics will no longer apply. That is to say, physics and the way we understand physics won't exist; but we are continually redefining physics. Without the burden of a three-dimensional body, you will not be subjected to physical pain or suffering. There may be a new realm of physics to deal with but we can only surmise.

Biblical scriptures have told us for thousands of years that man, in and within himself, could not overcome physics or sin. This is what precipitated the greatest sacrifice ever recorded in history. This sacrifice was Christ Himself, the son of the only Living God, giving His life for all of mankind; and His death can only provide your redemption.

It's not that you will overcome physics and sin any more than you can overcome gravity and fly over the Brooklyn Bridge. It will be because of the decisions you make when exposed to physics that will make the difference. It will also be because you try, which implies a fight to do right; and since you can't overcome it, you are covered by the blood of the greatest sacrifice ever given in history.

This is where drugs are the tool that is used to subvert, interrupt, and cause you to dismiss supernatural guidance. Even though Christ died for our sins, this still does not give us the right nor does it negate our responsibility to fight against physics and sin. It is obvious that man doesn't possess the willpower, stamina, integrity, or character to do this on his own. Just like a brave soldier on the battlefield who doesn't know the outcome, he doesn't have the right to run and leave his comrades and not fight.

If you really want eternity and you believe the scriptures, you must realize there is a big effort to subvert and prevent you from becoming part of this eternal plan. Many theologists and Biblical scholars will concur that even though Christ covered our sins, this doesn't give us a blank check to sin without an effort to repent. This would be tantamount to sacrificing Him over and over. This also doesn't mean we won't continue to sin. But it does mean we must continue to fight and resist. Lucky for us, when Christ gave His life and last breath on that cross, He forgave our past sins and the sins we haven't committed but will do so. If He can die for us, the least we can do is to continue to fight to our best ability.

It isn't that, after you accept salvation through Christ, you won't be challenged in every category or sin. It's how you will react that's supernatural. In a moment of road rage, if Christ lives in you, you're more likely to pull over and pray for a mad driver than reach for a gun.

The forces of good or evil create actions that become three-dimensional and have biological consequences. Murder, war, greed and jealousy are all created by a consciousness guided by a malevolent mind that is invisible. Love, compassion, understanding, forgiveness and charity are produced by a benevolent, loving mind. These two opposing forces appear to be somewhat balanced, or at least both are equally prevalent throughout history. We see this when we read history books or go back to the oldest Sumerian texts and Biblical history.

One theory is that the human mind or consciousness is the most perfect hard drive to have ever been created. Could it be possible that this hard drive can be downloaded in a nanosecond once death occurs? This is only hypothetical thinking, but it's very interesting when paired with modern possibilities. To say the least, this is interesting conjecture concerning the hereafter.

Of course, even in antiquity, human beings have always been fascinated about life after death, sometimes even more than we are today. One only has to look at the Egyptians; almost everything they did was to prepare for the afterlife.

There are so many examples, so much evidence, so many interesting facts that cannot be ignored about life after death. Now, modern science is even beginning to look for unconventional answers that prove there is a correlation between real science and Biblical teachings. For over a hundred years, science has struggled to prove that theology and religion have nothing to do with life. But it may have proved the opposite. Neurosurgeons, cardiologists, and scientists are more fascinated than ever with the possibility that we have more to look for after we die. It has been suggested by some that death itself may be just a trick or a matrix, and that dying isn't to be feared as much as we thought. Some now believe that death is just an illusion, a trip back to where your consciousness began.

We, as individuals, do not want to die. This is natural; no amount of words or logic could ever convince us we would be better off dead. Those who do commit suicide are influenced inside the consciousness by negative thoughts of hopelessness, which are often influenced by drugs or chemicals. This horrible desire to take one's own life is created by negative energy that perpetrates a lie stating that there is no hope.

One reason why it is quite often too late to help a suicidal person is because these negative energies are invisible. No one walks around with a sign on their back saying "Would you please help? I'm about to kill myself." But there are signs.

We are wired to put up a facade that everything is okay because of our egos, or to protect those we love. There may be dozens of reasons why a person would commit suicide, but every reason is created in a conscious mind. The decision to take one's life can come from a mind that's invisible, and that can be influenced with biological and supernatural consequences from drug use. That same mind that decided to end it all could have also been a positive force that could have saved lives as well as their own in the future. If drugs have caused this or if they are involved in a person's life, they will prevent good answers from saving you or someone you love.

A person's decision to shoot and kill 10 classmates or a father's decision to kill his own family was created in a vortex of sanity crowded with evil energy, usually because of a substance. Drugs are one of the most influential factors concerning crimes that were never before considered. The drug epidemic, in confluence with the legions of demons prophesied to be unleashed in this era, are the cause of the most bizarre murders occurring today.

One much overlooked trait that is associated with a crime is negative spiritual energy. Most in the medical or scientific world would agree because they can't see tangible evidence, only the results of my analysis. The truth is they are looking at the tangible evidence and consequences when they look at the bodies, but are still overlooking the cause. This is the same medical field that only treats symptoms instead of causes.

Science is now in the process of creating artificial intelligence. Nanotechnology is at the cutting edge, with results that may be forbidden for good reason. So far, nanotechnology is the closest thing that science can bring to bear that will work with human biology. That is to say, it's a scientific achievement similar to a human brain that can be engineered with trillions of non-biological cells or nanocells. If science had its way, these nanocells will communicate with each other, then self-perpetuate knowledge on their own without programming. This will allow these nanocells to replicate, reproduce and learn on their own, much like how our biological cells replicate.

Will science someday have the capability to capture every neuron's proximity to each other and instantly freeze them onto a data frame for later download? Could this data be downloaded into another piece of biology? Would these processes make it possible to recreate us mentally and emotionally to our exact status that existed right before death? If these questions sound like science fiction, it probably is. But anything that the human mind can imagine and conceive of will materialize eventually. This will require capturing the exact proximity of every neurotransmitter in the body at the second of death. Only now (because of nanotechnology) could science hope to give you another chance of continuity and life, with a new body.

This sci-fi scenario leaves out one important thing: the spiritual side of consciousness that is a part of the human creation. Then there are the scholars, scientists, and even some religions that believe that the spirit world doesn't contradict the world of science. In other words, there are those even in theological circles who believe that theology and science have parallels with no contradictions.

Mankind always strove to live for as long as possible, and to look as good as possible. I surmise that mankind will be prevented from accumulating knowledge that is forbidden. This knowledge is forbidden only while we exist in a three-dimensional world.

Other dimensions that will be available after death could offer all of the secrets to the universe.

This line of thinking isn't just hypothetical science, but is based on scriptures. Some theological scholars believe the Tower of Babel, where God confused the languages, was a disruption by God to stop knowledge and adjust a timeline. Without this interruption of knowledge, mankind may have achieved nuclear meltdown thousands of years ago.

This is not a religious book. However, one would be very naïve not to see the connections between drugs and recent history. One must ask at this point: How do drugs influence our creative side? One must also ask if drugs do create insight, and if they could kill millions. The Creator who placed the Earth in its exact distance from the sun so we could have a biosphere did not intend for man to breach a barrier of knowledge or time. The introduction of drugs into the human mind to ascertain knowledge often produces evil. Drugs can interrupt the original timeline and plan that God has for your eternity. Once man has qualified for eternity, all of the secrets of the universe will be revealed to a mind that is capable of understanding. It will also be a mind not contained or held back by physics.

This is spiritual reason and logic that we must trust and be patient for, unlike the fallen angels that did not do these things. Street drugs and pharmaceutical drugs can allow the human mind to open up demonic entities if they are used especially for this purpose. Evidence suggests in the Book of Enoch that these angels that were cast to Earth tried this early on, with destructive consequences for them and mankind.

Some scholars believe there are residual effects still occurring today from angelic transgressions with Earth women during the time of Enoch. In Matamoros, Mexico and other Texas border towns, these demonic actions and rituals are evident in the producers and transporters of drugs. Rituals and sacrifices along the Mexican border towns are the result of this drug trade perpetrated on American streets. There is an inordinate amount of demonic activity in this area fueled by drug sales; yes, they go hand in hand.

It is obvious that the substance we call drugs runs interference with sanity and logic. These drugs are the perfect tampering tool to influence the human psyche and mind. They are made available by the forces of evil opposite the forces of good. Evil or good are opposing forces: one produces evil and death, while the other produces goodness and life.

Some historians will tell you that without divine forces and supernatural intervention, mankind would have perished long ago. This supernatural intervention by a force of good from the God Family has often changed history. Astrophysicists and UFO buffs have strong evidence that missile silos have been prevented from launching nuclear warheads in times past. If this is true, I surmise this is another example of supernatural intervention by the God Family on man's behalf.

The crime, death, destruction, torture and evil slaughter of thousands in Mexico is a microcosm of what's happening in America. Each year, in the United States alone, almost 68,000 Americans died as a result of drug-related overdoses or crime. If you take into account the drug-related deaths that occurred in the last 40 years, you will see that we have lost more than in all wars combined. Never before has Satan had such a tool that allows him to perpetrate death and destruction upon mankind.

Man's decision-making process, which no other species has, implies he's being groomed for a much bigger role to play throughout the entire universe. This is the reason why he is the target of the drug cartel and the drug epidemic. After all, it has killed more in our nation than war and diseases. Man's capability to make decisions separates him from all other species. Throughout history, when species perish, it is either an act of nature, biology, or some other cataclysm.

Mexico's murders pale in comparison to those in Chicago and other American cities, but these are caused by drugs. Most of Mexico's murders are from turf wars. One could make the case that they are receiving their just reward for selling drugs. But that is a bad argument because the good die with the evil and even drug dealers can change, but most choose not to.

There is, of course, a more demonic plan being played out with the sale of drugs. Drugs are designed to destroy the flow of good chronological events and change time and space into death, destruction and evil. Yes, we're talking about the America that was originally founded, predicated and blessed because of its belief in God. Even our currency is used by coke dealers to snort cocaine, rolled up as a tool with the words "In God We Trust". Looking back at their drug use, this insult to injury has not been overlooked by those who have been addicted and are now well.

The objective of this book is to wake up America and the entire world. We will settle for America first. America is now a breeding ground that is capable of producing millions of dark souls. Two drugs alone are absolutely the rocket fuel that assist Satanic forces, and are the vehicles for evil driven and guided by Lucifer himself. Never before in American history have so many families been murdered by the very people they loved, trusted and counted on to protect them. The unpredictability of someone on meth or crack is as unpredictable as an earthquake in California. America, with its wealth and its belief in Christianity, is the reason why you are a target.

How many parents who love their children finally throw in the towel and quit trying to save that child from drugs? They quit trying because the person they were fighting for has become a demon or a monster. When evil forces hear those words from a parent, they realize they have surrendered. As a parent, you may never give up trying to save your child from this evil, but eventually may give out. The forces that are behind this evil are not biological nor three-dimensional, making it impossible to compete with them in a physical way.

Your Bible states that we wrestle against principles, not flesh and blood. Let's get one thing straight, America: You do not have a chance of saving your loved ones if you are not armed with intelligence and wisdom. This is also the reason why the scriptures tell us to put on the entire armor of God to fight these evil entities. This scripture is metaphorically speaking about characteristics like faith and Biblical intelligence when describing armor. Hopefully, this book has armored you with unconventional knowledge. This is wisdom that you can't seem to get in schools, or any of our universities.

America, we are bogged down by political correctness. We can't even stop and help each other on the side of the road anymore because of lawsuits and political correctness. In a direct way, we have passed more legislation to protect ourselves. These laws designed to protect us have put too much stress on our society.

At the end of World War II, America was a society that could communicate with and help each other in times of need without fear of reprisal or a lawsuit. Americans could also talk to each other without being offended by the use of words. We are now a nation of cynics, skeptics and liars, with little trust among ourselves. Drugs are destroying our character and logic that are our only real possessions. All of the crime perpetrated by drugs has forced us into a shell and made us hide behind steel doors and burglar bars.

America, you can thank some in the medical field and our legislators who allowed drugs to cross our borders for 60 years. In the '50s and '60s, the average American could actually go to bed and usually leave his door open or unlocked. It is dangerous to go to bed in Chicago, Dallas or Houston now without a knife, a gun and a bodyguard.

In an effort to tiptoe through the tulips and not offend anyone, we have handicapped and handcuffed our educational systems from success. Our entire educational system is prevented from creating good results in their students because of political correctness. A teacher reprimanding or punishing a student who is hurting himself and the class now results in her dismissal or jail time. Teachers can no longer reprimand or correct a student to make them smarter without fear of being called conservative and biased. Often, a teacher will be accused of racism or bigotry for trying to better a person.

America is forced to import great minds from other countries like nuclear physicists, microbiologists and astrophysicists because of drugs and political correctness. Although they're smart, they don't share our long-term political interests and are changing a generation to think like them. While America is critiquing our phrases and splitting hairs with words, our children are buying and dying from black tar heroin and fentanyl.

Conclusion

After reading this book, you will fight for yourself, your loved ones, and your country. You will be a part of an overall larger fight to save America. Hopefully you will be part of the solution. If you are one of the millions who have an addiction small or large, this book will break the chains and make sense of how it occurred in your life.

This chapter will be dedicated to pointing out techniques, attitudes and therapies. These solutions are not predicated on drugs.

If you are successful in defeating your addiction, it will be incumbent upon you to share your wisdom with others who are suffering from the same problem. If you use this knowledge to save others even though you aren't addicted, you will be a part of something much greater than you can ever imagine. If you do lose someone because of drugs after you fought hard, it will give you comfort later. Don't listen to those who tell you not to get involved, or the person will straighten up when they are ready. We now know they don't.

It is true that some drug users and alcoholics finally have enough if they're still alive. Timing is important in this fight to save yourself or to rescue someone else you love. The timing is indeed tricky: if you try too soon or don't try soon enough, it could backfire. If you don't try at all, I guarantee that it will backfire.

These are uncharted waters for America. We didn't deal with this or any other epidemic for the first 200 years of our history. Only in the last 60 years has this curse devastated the masses. What we know today is far greater than 40 years ago. This common sense and knowledge is evolving and unfolding week by week and year by year. Unfortunately, we are learning only because of the deaths. We have nothing to compare this to, no parallels that match our culture or the losses we have and will continue to incur.

If you are trying to get off drugs, start by realizing how bad things could be instead of how bad things are. You could be in prison, physically scarred for life, or even mutilated as a result of the violence connected to the drug culture. You would be surprised by how many drug users, even young people, end up in nursing homes like old people for the rest of their lives. This is due to strokes, heart attacks and other ailments, car wrecks or violence as a result of drug use.

Never lose this perspective; and always remember your friends, acquaintances and even relatives who have died. When you're thinking of those who have perished, ask yourself: Could they have stopped, and were they given help and patience?

Be grateful that you have come to a place in your mind where you recognize and appreciate that you are about to change. This attitude will be the rocket fuel that will create success. Attitude will be the first step mentally, followed by more mental and emotional adjustments, tweaks and changes.

Once you have your attitude right and you have decided that you will not be defeated or distracted by blaming others, you are on a good road to recovery. Look around at your life, and accept it for what it is. If you live in the past, you will drown in your own regrets.

At this point, every step you take forward will be a step away from darkness and a step toward light and good health. This new you is your baby; you are going to be the one who rocks it. You are going to be the one who has to endure the depression, physical pain, and feelings of guilt; but only for a short time. You will be the one who reaps the rewards and peace of mind that comes with knowing where you're going.

The good part of owning this responsibility is that you have knowledge under your belt that many people in your circle, even family members, would never dream or know about. Your street smarts are something you paid for with hard lessons; you might as well use it. It doesn't matter what people think. It's still your life and your choice to live. There's something honorable and rewarding in knowing you have decided to own it and it was your screw-up.

The moment you reach this level of thinking, you will feel as if a 600-pound gorilla has been lifted from your back, and you will feel free like never before. This will create a euphoria of dignity and success that isn't induced by drugs, but by something good that you did. This will make you feel like a positive, worthy, and useful part of mankind. This will be the opposite of using drugs, which makes you feel guilty, sad and depressed; and takes away your dignity. It may take years for someone to alter the natural chemicals in the brain, but they will finally return and rebalance.

Most of all, be patient. Always remember how worse off you could be, and never look back. The great things that will come out of this are wisdom and longevity that will enable you to pass it to the next generation. This is called the circle of life. This circle of life is exactly the opposite of the circle of death that we covered in a previous chapter.

Sometimes, in life, it's hard to believe that something good can come out of anything so horrible. The truth is if you study history, you will discover that this is always what made for a better world. It is possible for you to make quantum leaps and catch up emotionally, physically, spiritually and financially.

Most of us have heard or used this expression: "You've never really lived until you've almost died." Since your drug use is history and behind you in a linear sense, this will allow you to share wisdom as you travel life's road. Those years of drug abuse, disappointments and abuse perpetrated by you will be in your rear-view mirror as you enter the future. It will also be a road you will never travel again with knowledge. You lived, and millions didn't.

The one thing that all human beings share is a three-dimensional body, something we also mentioned in earlier chapters. This makes us all subject to the same laws of physics. The body that you possess is, quite literally, God-given. It belongs to you, and it's your responsibility to keep it clean.

There are thousands of ways and much research you will want to do to find ways to make your body better. Some of the things are obvious and fundamental, such as good eating habits, exercise, and a positive mindset. When you begin to do research on health and exercise, you will turn a negative into a positive.

If you were addicted to opiates or any other drug, something interfered with the naturally flowing chemicals in your brain known as endorphins. These endorphins are responsible for the way you feel about yourself and your self-esteem, as well as your physical status. When you were on drugs and in the process of abusing yourself, they were not released. And even if they were, you would not have recognized them.

Chocolate and sunshine are both extremely effective in the fight against opiates, but there are lots of natural things that you are going to want to research. Apparently, they are not endorsed by rehabs. But ask anyone who's been an addict, and they would agree. Endorphins are prevented from being released when you're on drugs. Opiates particularly prevent this from happening. When you are clean and sober and if you are weightlifting, jogging, swimming, or engaged in any sport or hobby, your brain releases endorphins. "Runner's high" is a naturally occurring high that happens after 15 or 20 minutes of light jogging or running. Your choice of exercise is totally up to you. The best part is when you share the experience with others. It inspires you and those who may have had similar problems.

By taking care of your body, you will receive compliments from people after a few weeks that will inspire you, and this will be a self-perpetuating process. (Some workouts produce more compliments than others. I personally believe weightlifting and bodybuilding are the greatest workouts.) This allows you to take the results of your training everywhere you go—after all, you don't go anywhere without your body. After a few weeks, you will begin to wonder why it took so long for you to start, and why you didn't start sooner. Always remember: better late than never, better sooner than later.

Rehabs won't push this narrative. Their solution: mind-bending drugs that will control your behavior. Rehabs want to tether you to the pharmaceutical industry for the rest of your life. Their place concerning the drug epidemic is in initial detox, which can be helpful but can't be the end result. Their facilities are run by a very narrow-minded and stubborn group of professionals who will not leave the pharmaceutical industry out of your life. Most of you know that the pharmaceutical industry began your drug use. This will be the first attempt by rehabs to bring people back into the drug culture. Some of these professionals know this means job security.

These so-called rehabs just want to leave you dependent on drugs because it keeps you reliant on them. They are good at recognizing why you're there, but they are terrible at keeping you from coming back. You come into this world alone. Your parents take care of you until your teenage years are over, and then you are on your own. Rehabs are not your parents. You have to think logically and intelligently, and not tether yourself to the same system that put you there to begin with.

I am not telling you not to go to rehab. At some point, you should; and you should listen and cooperate. Most drug users will never get to the point of just reading this book, getting the answers and then changing in order to save their lives. Rehab is a necessity at first, but then it's time to look for alternatives that make you both cured and permanently free of drugs.

The changes you will want to make to prevent relapse will be anywhere from a change of location or even joining the military. If you have been in jail or prison for some time, the very worst thing you can do is to go home. Your parents, siblings and friends mean well when they tell you they can't wait to cook you a big meal, hug you, and go to a movie with you like nothing ever happened. They are innocent, but they are wrong. If you've been on drugs like meth and you return to the same town, home or neighborhood or go near these places, you will be back in jail shortly. It doesn't matter how adamant you are upon returning home; it will happen, especially when you try not to screw up or cope with finding a job, or experience a little stress.

As I stated in an earlier chapter, evil Satanic forces will make sure that the stage is set for drugs to find you, especially when you don't want them. Only someone who has been on drugs will realize how right I am about that last statement, and they can all remember what I'm talking about. Family members and friends don't believe or just don't recognize these evil forces that are trying to take your life.

This is a reason for you not to go home for a while. When you go back to the same 'hood, the connections are still there. The dealers and friends you were buying from and doing drugs with could still be there; or many could have gone to jail and been released, or are now deceased. Some could be back on the streets, doing drugs and counting on you to join them because they know your problem. Suddenly, because of you trying too hard or your boredom and impatience, you will fall. It's game over; even a small amount will end hope. At this time, you don't need old friends or contacts. When you get anywhere from 500 miles or further away from home, you have a better chance at success. Connections are not made overnight in drug culture.

It is true that you can go out looking for it, and you know what to look for on the streets if you really want drugs. But you don't really want drugs at this point, or you would not have moved 500 miles away. The time you put in and the effort required from you will ensure the moment will pass. To make these drugs plentiful and in your face requires familiarity, and you don't fit that profile in a new town. This will help remove the temptation and availability that you just don't need right now. This will also add time to your sobriety: every minute, hour, day and week spent clean and sober will make you stronger. You will soon be like a cancer patient who's never really lived until they've almost died. You will soon be free, and put this bad season of your life even further behind.

This is also the reason why you should ask the judge in your case to parole you to another town, if probation is a part of your release. As a repeat drug offender, this should not be something you have to request. The court systems should make it a requirement that if you're a repeat offender, you have to be paroled to a faraway location.

Law enforcement and the American judicial system have a lot to learn about drug rehabilitation. Releasing a person right back to the same neighborhood guarantees failure. This occurs so probation officers can watch them. Yes, it's job security for them, not success for you. This is where they are doing the wrong thing: if they really wanted success, they would reverse that and demand you not go near home for at least one year, except for a short and supervised visit.

Some of you will not even have to go to jail, and may get off of drugs with the help of the military. If your body hasn't gone too far, if your criminal record isn't too bad, and with just a small amount of reasonable education, you can qualify. This, of course, will have the same effect as you not going back to your own hometown because you will be traveling abroad for Uncle Sam. You will be on the right track and the right train, and this train will be traveling at the speed of life instead of the speed of death.

Eddie Delon Baker

References

"Blitzkrieg". The History Channel. Retrieved on March 12, 2019 from https://www.history.com/topics/world-war-ii/blitzkrieg.

"JFK Assassination Reports and Records". The Assassination Archives and Research Center. Retrieved March 12, 2019 from http://www.aarclibrary.org/publib/contents/contents_jfk.htm.

Shapira, Ian. "Trump delays full release of some JFK assassination files until 2021, bowing to national security concerns". *The Washington Post*, April 27, 2018. Retrieved March 12, 2019 from https://www.washingtonpost.com/news/retropolis/wp/2018/04/26/trump-delays-release-of-some-jfk-files-until-2021-bowing-to-national-security-concerns/.